THE MISADVENTURES OF
MR BADSHOT

THE **MISADVENTURES** OF **MR BADSHOT**

CHARLES FOSTER
Illustrated by James Wade

First published in the UK in 2010
by Quiller, an imprint of Quiller Publishing Ltd

British Library Cataloguing-in-Publication Data
A catalogue record for this book
is available from the British Library

ISBN 978 1 84689 082 6

Book and cover design by Sharyn Troughton
Printed in China

Quiller
An imprint of Quiller Publishing Ltd
Wykey House, Wykey, Shrewsbury, SY4 1JA
Tel: 01939 261616 Fax: 01939 261606
E-mail: info@quillerbooks.com
Website: www.countrybooksdirect.com

CONTENTS

AUTHOR'S PREFACE

MICK BADSHOT IS REAL. He lives in the Somerset Levels in a traumatised village that should not be hard to identify. He drinks at the Halfway House at Pitney, the Bell Inn at Curry Mallet, and the Canal Inn at Wrantage. I am very fond of him, but he is a disaster.

He appears every month in the *Shooting Times*. I suggested to the *Shooting Times* that the sporting press is unrealistically triumphalist. It is full of stories about effortlessly long shots, huge bags and smooth expeditions. That's not my experience, and it is not Mick's. He puts the record straight, and his own and everyone's nose out of joint.

James Wade has his character just right, but (entirely deliberately, to save the real Mick's blushes) the face isn't quite the same, and the real Mick's paunch isn't quite so big.

Although I wouldn't like to live there all the time, I like Mick's world. I enjoy re-entering it every month. It is a romantic, optimistic swashbuckling world, where hope and cussedness triumph continually over experience, common sense, physics and the rules of accountancy. He's a dreaming Pickwickian maverick, full of pork pies and doomed schemes; sensitive, touchy, unbiddable, infuriating and fun. My life would be a lot poorer without him, and I hope very much that you get on with him too.

Charles Foster
Oxford
March 2010

ILLUSTRATOR'S PREFACE

WHEN ASKED BY THE AUTHOR to contribute a preface summarising the illustrator's reactions to Mr Badshot, my first thought was that I would rather draw ten pictures than write one word, and my second was a sense of relief that at least two good-sized counties intervene between the Somerset Levels and Shropshire, my own county of residence. Even so, I have come to enjoy observing Badshot's exploits from afar as the seasons have come and gone and one disaster has followed another. Each month when the cry comes across the office, 'Another Badshot for you, James!' I know that the next evening or two will need to be spent in his company.

It is not usually difficult to select the scene to be illustrated, the rule being that Mr Badshot is always the focus in one or other of his numerous manifestations. Occasionally there are other characters too irresistible to ignore – Mrs Grout and the Animal Analyst being notable examples.

Each illustration starts with a very free pencil sketch which is then tightened up by tracing onto greaseproof paper raided from the kitchen drawer. It is then reversed and transferred onto cartridge paper. This means that Mr Badshot always starts life as a left-hander with buttons that fasten the wrong way. The earlier illustrations were inked using Rotring pen, but as these have clogged and dried up I have resorted to a dip pen and Indian ink. A fountain pen is occasionally used for reinforcement. The finishing touch is a light colour wash using a well-worn set of Caran D'ache crayons.

James St Clair Wade
Shrewsbury
March 2010

ACKNOWLEDGEMENTS

WE ARE VERY GRATEFUL to all the editorial staff at the *Shooting Times* for their interest in Mick Badshot's exploits, for their efficiency in getting him out into the world every month, and for their permission to reproduce this account of his life.

Andrew Johnston of Quiller has been tremendous. He took to Mick from the start, and has been encouraging and enthusiastic ever since. There are no more congenial publishers.

But most of all we have to thank the real Mick: he is CF's best friend and brother-in-arms.

I.

BADSHOT AND SAMURAI

'IT'S DISCIPLINE YOU NEED IN A DOG', said Mick. 'Discipline and balls. And Mrs Grout has both.' He meant, I hoped, that Mrs Grout had dogs with both, but it was still with queasy misgivings that I went with him to see.

Mrs Grout lived in a bleak, pebble-dashed eyrie jammed right up against the sea wall. My memory insists that it was called Buggaov Hall, but that can't be right. Salt spray had rusted the barbed wire entanglements that lined the drive, and a sign on the gate showed a mangled burglar in a man-trap. By the door, eating thistles, was a mournful three-legged goat that had presumably wandered absent-mindedly into Mrs Grout's minefield. The Grout coat of arms was up over the porch: a white rabbit being savaged by a couple of stoats.

Mick took a deep breath and pulled the bell pull. From inside the echoing house a tidal wave of noise crashed towards us. Bodies thudded against the door. Noses and feet were pushed through the letter box. Then a deep voice sang out: 'Silence', and the world was still. The noses froze in the letter box. Milk curdled in distant dairies.

There was a great unbolting, the door swung open, and there stood Mrs Grout, in a sea of dogs. She was in one of those tweed skirts that would take the skin off your hand if you were brave enough to stroke it. She had brogues like battleships, thighs like beech boles, and Brunel must have made her bra out of armour-piercing steel. Her face was scarlet with broken veins and colonial outrage. Her upper lip was making a fair stab at a full cavalry moustache. She held a mug of Horlicks in one hand and a Webley service revolver in the other. The walls behind her were covered with the bodies of animals that she had speared or strangled in distant outposts of Empire.

'Come in,' she boomed, disappointed that we weren't the unwanted tradesmen she'd been after for weeks. And so we did.

She bred, she said, the hardiest black labs on the planet. 'See him?', she said, pointing to a puppy the size of a skip, slumped by the Aga, chewing on an apparently human femur. 'His ancestors were Anglo-Saxon Marsh Dogs. They were never fed, but lived on herons and escaped convicts. It's said that they delayed the Viking invasion of Northumbria by a good half-century.' Mick looked at the dog open-mouthed. She went on: 'I took his mother to field trials when she was in pup. When the shot was fired, all the foetuses in the litter jumped, but this one – I'm sure it was this one – somehow knew where the dummy had landed and lurched towards it in the womb.'

In an infatuated daze Mick wrote out a huge cheque. Mrs Grout tucked it into the rhino's scrotum where she kept the petty cash. 'We've ripped her off,' whispered Mick, as we walked back to the Land Rover, leading the dog. 'I feel bad about it, really.'

Throughout the summer Mick, happy as Larry, threw dummies into ponds and practised his whistles. He watched training videos and bought drinks for the people from the Gundog Scurry at the Game Fair. He called the dog Samurai: 'It's his unquestioning obedience and his martial qualities, you see.' Then on the first day of the season, with all Mick's friends told to expect wonders, Samurai was ready to go.

Knowing Mick's shooting as I do, I thought that Samurai was likely to die of old age without getting nearer a mouthful of feathers than the pillow he'd wrecked at the curate's. But I did Mick an injustice. His first shot of the day winged the slowest, unluckiest, most suicidal and most diseased pheasant in Somerset. Samurai bounded off to retrieve it. Mick started some very complex whistling. The bird sat up and looked the dog resentfully in the eye.

I would never have credited Samurai with such astonishing speed over rough ground. To go that fast with his tail firmly between his legs was a testimony to his Spartan roots. It must have hurt like hell. We found him two days later eating broccoli from a bin bag in Ilminster. He's a kind, gentle animal, philosophically vegan, and he hates fresh air. He won't go out of the house except to trot after Mick along the supermarket aisles. 'He's very biddable round Asda', insists Mick. So that's all right then.

2.

BADSHOT,
FIELD SPORTS EVANGELIST

'THE TROUBLE WITH TODAY'S YOUTH', said Mick to the people in the Halfway House who hadn't been quick enough to bolt for the back bar when he came in, 'is that they're brainwashed. They're not individuals. They're moulded by the mass media, and the mass media lives in Fulham and loathes and fears the countryside.'

We all nodded, and wondered where this was leading. Mick had a strange, fanatical light in his eyes. We'd all seen it before, and it usually meant humiliation or serious personal injury for him and his friends.

'Something has to be done. Time is running out. And if we don't act now we'll lose the war against the forces of urban darkness, and lose the souls of a generation.' This was a man with a passion. His hand trembled and his knuckles whitened around his pint of cider. He reached into his jacket, pulled out a grubby piece of paper, and laid it on the bar. 'Look at this,' he said, conspiratorially. We all looked obediently over his shoulder. 'This is a list of the primary schools in the Somerset Levels. Each represents a magnificent opportunity either for Us or for Them: for Salvation or for Destruction.' We all heard the capital letters, and looked nervously for the exits. 'We must take the Word out to the nations.'

The Word, it seemed, was the message that field sports were crucial to the health of the countryside. We all devoutly agreed with that. But we had deeply devout doubts about whether Mick had been anointed to preach it. He plainly saw himself as the Billy Graham of the hunting and shooting world. He had an unshakeable belief in his calling. 'You might think that someone in denim and more in touch with the younger generation ought to be doing this,' he said. We all did, but bit our tongues until they bled into our beer. 'You might think that children will only listen to someone dressed in MP3s.' We all winced and wished he'd researched rather better. 'But let me tell you,' he went on, unabashed; 'experience and integrity convince where relentless coolness will not. I'm the man to call the Levels back to the Land.' He'd clearly been working hard on this last flourish, and looked expectantly round for appreciation. We looked hard and silently into our glasses.

'We have to stop him,' said Mervyn, on the way home. 'We owe it to our children and our grandchildren.' But Mick was a hard man to stop.

The insane grandeur of his plans became clear over the next few weeks. He mailed all the schools on his list, offering to come and do 'Countryside Assemblies'. If the headteacher didn't reply in a fortnight, he put on his tweed shooting suit, yellow garters and his old BFSS tie, went to the school in person and asked nicely for a response. If the response was a 'no', things started to get nasty. He dressed up as a fox and stood at the school entrance with a mock gin trap on his leg, moaning in a vaguely vulpine sort of way to emphasise how miserable the hunting ban had been for foxes, and handing out to terrified seven-year olds brochures saying: 'Foxy's leg hurts. Please let poor Foxy tell his story.' He was soon the oldest person in the village to have an ASBO. He was delighted. 'It'll give me huge credibility with the drug-crazed teenagers,' he said.

The real horrors, though, were reserved for those children unfortunate enough to go to those (very few) schools who had been bamboozled into letting Mick run an assembly.

These dreadful occasions started with Mick bounding onto the stage in a dog costume and breathily telling his audience how he (a foxhound called Nigel) was redundant and was terrified of being shot. Nigel periodically lifted his leg and urinated against a post in his nervousness. Then followed a PowerPoint demonstration linking the closure of rural post offices with the demise of otter hunting, and to top it all, a short but graphic black and white film of a massive pre-war pheasant shoot in Norfolk, complete with beaters doffing their caps to Purdey-wielding toffs with handlebar moustaches. The final frame was a still photo of hundreds of dead birds surrounded by spaniels and beaming aristocrats. 'There you see it,' said Mick, brightly. 'The country needs country sports.' There was silence, broken by occasional sobs, and Mick was ushered quickly to the door.

'Some of our kids will be in therapy for life,' a teacher told a local newspaper. And a spokesman for the League Against Cruel Sports, with a bolt through his cheek, smugly reported an unprecedented surge in applications for family membership.

'I've had tremendously encouraging media attention,' said Mick, back in the Halfway House, to the empty bar.

3.

BADSHOT'S WOLDS WOE

IT ALL STARTED WELL ENOUGH. The pub had proper beer, a chap on the table next to us choked amusingly on a dry roasted peanut, the beds were hard and there was no TV. In the morning we were gung-ho over the black pudding. This wasn't really sport, said Mick, who knew about these things. The Lincolnshire wolds were the pigeon-shooters' mecca. You just had to point your barrels vaguely skyward, pull the trigger, and then duck to avoid being stunned by the avalanche of bodies that would cascade out of the sky. But it was good for guns to get really hot once in a while, and today, said Mick, he would be wearing asbestos gloves. Our barrels would glow red like the volley-firing Martini Henry rifles on the stockade at Rourke's Drift.

Mick had a little book in which he planned his campaigns. The wind, according to the shipping forecast, would be south-westerly. That meant that we should lay out our decoys in a fan pattern at the corner of the stubble by the big elms. Most of the birds would land about twenty-five yards from our hide. It was all mapped out. Our approach to the dyke where we would lie was marked with blue arrows: the flight of the birds was in red. He had thought of everything. He had even told the local game dealer to cancel all leave and have an army of experienced pluckers warmed up and ready to go.

We felt a bit wistful as we set off in the Land Rover. Big bag days like this were the sort of thing that gave shooting a bad name. The joy of shooting, we told one another over the tape of *633 Squadron* on the stereo, was not about disc-rupturing hauls of birds, but about days in the open air, listening to thrushes, watching the wind in the trees and having our thumbs on the pulse of the English seasons.

I had thought of Lincolnshire as being flat and placid. It was flat enough, but there was nothing remotely placid about it. I couldn't hear a single thrush above the thunderous flapping of pigeon wings as the flights came into our decoys, or sense the throb of the seasons above Mick's foul language as he realised that he had left all our cartridges in Somerset.

4.

BADSHOT, ECO-WARRIOR

'IT'S DISGUSTING,' said Mick, 'the way we're despoiling the planet. There was a good pound of brass cases in the dashboard. And I just chucked them away.' Mick had been to an Eco-Fair in a flooded field. And there, amongst the wind-chimes and the hemp yoghurt stalls, Mick got religion. 'The Earth is our mother,' he told me, over a pint of organic beer demanded from a mystified barman. 'And mothers deserve respect.'

Mick's way of respecting his mother was to turn to home-loading. 'I will never fire another cartridge that I haven't loaded myself. It will be good for my self-respect, and good for the polar ice caps.' So he set up a little factory in the barn and sat up into the early hours ramming and crimping. He oozed sanctimonious pride.

A fox was causing havoc. It had taken two hens a week from Mick's little pen, and Mick was getting wild. 'It's reducing our ability to be self-sufficient,' he said. 'We might be forced to buy eggs. And that would encourage greenhouse gas emissions.' So, with lots of talk about the importance of ploughing foxes back into the carbon cycle, that fox was sentenced to death.

Under the transparent pretence of making a tree house for the children, Mick had built a high seat at the end of the field. It commanded

16

splendid views over the plough and the hen run. 'Tonight,' said Mick, 'is the night of nemesis.'

So he blacked his face and put on camouflage so efficient that he had no idea where his legs were. We climbed together into the high seat. I saw his profile against the darkening horizon. It was the sort of profile you see in those boys' Commando comics: grim, square-jawed, determined and deadly. He started doing his rabbit squealing noise and the fox, which had clearly never heard a real rabbit squeal, started to move in. There was a reasonable moon, and we could see him creep up the dyke towards us. Mick stopped squealing and picked up the rifle. The fox looked disappointed – presumably thinking the rabbit had died or escaped. But having come this way, he must have thought, he might as well make something of the night. So he turned in towards the hens.

That hen run was supposed to be impregnable. On top of the high chicken wire fence was a strand of electric fencing with the current turned up full: 'That'll teach him,' Mick had said. Chicken wire was buried several feet deep to prevent burrowing.

But somehow the fox got in. 'It's his last spree,' whispered Mick, as he levelled the rifle. The safety catch clicked off. 'Now,' said Mick to me. I turned the spotlight on. There was the fox, fine and insolent. 'Goodbye,' said Mick, and squeezed the trigger.

There was a click. Then a pause, a curse, and a rapid reloading. Mick squeezed again. Again a click. The fox looked contemptuously at us, turned around, grabbed one of the precious Marran hens that by now were frantic, and started to trot away, the hen still flapping in his mouth.

Mick moved with a speed that was a credit to his muesli and lentil diet. He was down the ladder in a flash and racing towards the pen brandishing the .22 like a club.

I will never forget the blood curdling scream that rang out, or the sight of Mick writhing on the electric fence with all that current pulsing through his gonads. There was something unearthly and primeval about it.

It was the last we heard of the environment. Next morning Mick waddled painfully to the breakfast table, pushed aside his papaya porridge and asked for sausages. And the shares in the cartridge companies must have soared over the next month.

5.

BADSHOT GOES BACK TO NATURE

'WE'RE DIVORCED FROM OUR CELTIC ROOTS,' said Mick, who was sitting in a newly acquired kaftan cleaning his 12 bore. 'I'm part of that wood. The trees are my brothers and the flowers are my sisters.'

We all sighed. He had phases like this. They didn't last long, but they usually ended in tears. 'I'm off to the wood this summer. I'll live there, eat what I can shoot and gather, and I'll get properly tuned in again.' We nodded enthusiastically. He was best out of the house until the madness left him.

Whatever you say about Mick (and we said a lot that day), he's a man of his word. He was off that afternoon with a billhook, a sleeping bag, some packets of water purifying tablets, a couple of guns and enough ammunition to have changed the outcome of Trafalgar. 'Goodbye,' he said, as he trudged off up the lane. 'See you at the autumn solstice.'

We expected to see him slink shamefacedly back for dinner, but we had misjudged the man. He wasn't back that night, or the night after that. In fact we didn't see him for a week. We sometimes thought that we heard a shot from the wood, or saw smoke spiralling above the elms. We began to envy him. It was glorious weather. The swallows dived over the meadow and the swifts screamed over the high pinnacles of Mick's wood. The wood pigeons were fat and I could imagine them sizzling in Mick's pan. The rabbits were huge and abundant, and I wouldn't have minded toasting them over beech wood in the gloaming.

So I decided to visit Mick. I knew where he'd be. He'd often said that he'd like to live under the bank where we waited pointlessly for pigeons. There was a stream there, and a matchless view of the Levels.

He'd been there, sure enough. He'd made a shelter on a skeleton of elm branches, thatched it with big sycamore leaves and straw stolen from a nearby barn. It wasn't a bad effort. His latrine was a good deal more obvious than that of the badgers who shared his bank. There was a fire place, but none of the charred rabbit bones I'd expected. And there was no sign of Mick.

It took us another week of detective work to run him to ground. I burst in on him as he lay spreadeagled on his bed in the local motel. He was reading a book about SAS survival techniques, the room was ankle deep in Ferrero Rocher wrappers, and instead of the shame you'd expect, he boasted that he'd got the place at half rate and the lasagne was first rate.

6.

BADSHOT, BUCKSMAN

MICK KNOWS A LOT ABOUT ROE STALKING. I know this because he's always telling us. His shelves groan with American books called things like *How to whip them bucks' asses real good* and German books with reams of tables showing you how your bullet's trajectory varies the ambient temperature, your cat's birthday and your aunt's sexual orientation. His gun cabinet, ominously bolted to the wall with rivets salvaged from the *Titanic*, is full of highly polished weapons, all for highly specific uses. 'This .243 here,' said Mick, 'is zeroed to 115 yards. It's ideal for large mid-season muntjac.' He stroked it lovingly. 'And this .308: it's perfect for the smaller kudu you run into just after the rains in east-central Botswana.' But nothing, in Mick's experience, could touch the excitement of high summer roe stalking in the Quantocks. 'We're off there tonight,' he said. 'Come along.' And so I did.

Well, it was glorious up there. The fields glowed, and so did we. We walked a bit from the Land Rover, spied a roebuck on the opposite side of a deep coombe, and began a convoluted approach that would have made a Sioux hunter burst into ecstasies of professionally admiring applause. 'Grass in the wind,' whispered Mick theatrically, 'often misleads. It's too *local* to be useful.' We were lying prone in a patch of thistles about 300 yards from the buck. He hoisted some sort of computerised wind speed and direction meter on a huge telescopic aerial. The branch it brought crashing down stunned Mick and sent the buck racing off across a road. There was a screech of brakes, but sadly not in time.

I happened to see Mick's Game Book entry in relation to that evening. It didn't actually say that the buck had been felled with a brilliant running shot from a kneeling position, but it didn't say that it wasn't. 'Roe Buck: Nigel's Bottom. 300 yards,' it said. I thought it was a bit strange that the buck was sent off to the taxidermist, and now has pride of place in Mick's study. But not as strange as the absence of any other roe heads, now that I think about it.

'Mick?' said the stalker unkindly. 'He's got three ways of culling deer. He erodes them bit by bit, he kills them from lead-poisoning, or he waits until they're so old that a bang gives them a heart attack.' Not only was he unkind, but I happen to know he was wrong.

7.

BADSHOT GOES FERRETING

'FERRETING'S THE WAY FORWARD,' Mick announced one night. 'I need new challenges.' My heart sank, as it always does when Mick gets a great new idea. I had complete faith in his ability to turn the simplest enterprise into a life-endangering catastrophe.

He knew nothing about ferrets. The only time I'd seen him with one was when he tried to get one to act as a pull-through for his punt gun. 'Country solutions,' he'd said, tapping his head sagely. He'd put the ferret in at the breech and then stood for an hour waving an open can of catfood by the muzzle, hoping to get it to gallop through. It decided to set up home half-way down the barrel and Mick had had to flush it out with a bucket of cold water. But that was a while ago, the animal cruelty charges were dropped, and Mick had been reading up on ferrets since then.

'Watch this,' he said one night at The Canal, taking some baler twine and a small marlin spike from his pocket. The girls at the bar stood amazed as, with a deft wrist movement, clearly born of hours of practice, he produced a perfect couple of links of purse net. 'I'm making all my own kit,' he said, and my foreboding grew.

He made a hutch to a design he'd found in a Victorian boys' book, bought a couple of jills from an ad in the newsagent, and was ready to go. 'Come with me, will you?' he said. 'I'll need some help carrying all the rabbits home.' So we went out one glorious summer evening and pegged out his splendid homemade nets at a huge warren on the edge of the wood. So far so good.

Mick took his prize jill, Doreen, from a bag, prised her teeth out of his hand and put her to one hole. She took a sniff and bolted into the wood. I presume she is still living happily there. Mick grunted stoically and took out his second jill, Eileen. Eileen was plainly a natural rabbiter. She was down the hole like a shot. There were satisfying sounds of stampeding underground. We drew back to watch the nets. Eileen did her work well. Sure enough, a big rabbit came careering out into a net. The net stretched, and then a very odd thing happened. The rabbit went into dramatic reverse and was catapulted back at high speed towards the hole. It met Eileen coming out, and knocked her out cold. The rabbit, non-plussed, lolloped over Eileen's stunned body back into the warren.

There was an inquest, of course. It turned out that Mick had made his nets out of high tensile elastic string. Eileen won't go anywhere near a hole and will only sleep with the lights on. 'Ferreting's overrated,' said Mick, and sold his nets at a car boot sale.

8.

BADSHOT
ON THE FORESHORE

AT LAST MICK'S NAME came to the top of the waiting list for the Wildfowling Club. With the energy of a be-tweeded tsunami he threw himself into the business of learning the arcane tricks of the wildfowler's trade. He cut out cardboard silhouettes of all the major ducks and geese and stuck them to the ceiling above his head. He made a frieze out of duck pictures and swung at them with an air rifle when he was sitting at his desk. A CD of whistling teal and honking greylags was on continuous (and deeply irritating) loop in the Land Rover. He spent hours floundering round in a ditch at the bottom of his garden, allegedly perfecting his hide-making techniques, and he impregnated his decoys with synthetic duck pheromones from Minnesota. He bought drinks for everyone at the pub meetings of the Club, sitting reverently as they talked about the right loads for Canadas and the merits and demerits of neoprene and rubber waders. He made no secret of his ambitions: a specially commissioned carving on the stock of his pristine Beretta semi-auto showed him crouching in a trench, an unmistakably smug look on his Camo-creamed face as dozens of pole-axed geese crashed into the marsh all around him.

Soon he had firm and highly mathematical views on the ballistics of tungsten matrix and steel. He covered beer-mats with graphs demonstrating the comparative lethalities (his word, from an Oregon gun catalogue) of the 12 bore and the 8 bore. Many a menu was ruined by elaborate diagrams showing the place of mid-winter widgeon in the ecological web of the Somerset coast. He had a vast library of Victorian wildfowlers' reminiscences, all flagged up with little yellow Post-It notes, and had hung a map of the Wash over his desk so that he could follow the stories more accurately. He asked the local primary school if they would be interested in a talk about the regrettable demise of punt-gunning. He'd even be happy to deliver it in an authentic Norfolk accent, he said, but curiously the headmaster couldn't find a date for it.

Nothing was left to chance. 'There's no use having a marvellous eye and the stealth of an Apache if your dog lets you down,' he modestly told a glassy-eyed congregation at the Halfway House, one very long Friday night. 'My dog's in top physical and mental form.'

What he meant by this, it turned out, was that the CD had been piped into the kennel, the dog had been trained with dummies smeared with mallard fat, and, to accustom them both to the rigours of life beyond the sea wall, they had taken cold baths together every night. This raised a few jaded eyebrows, and someone choked on a pickled egg. But Mick was undaunted: 'Not that cold acclimatisation is necessary, of course. Technology does it all.' That same Oregon catalogue, apparently, sold silicon spray for dogs. 'A few puffs of that,' Mick assured us, 'and the dog'll be as waterproof and as cosy as an otter.'

The day came. The alarm clock went off on the dot of three. We blearily ate some breakfast, put all the kit in the car, and drove off to the marsh. We were going to a little island a short walk across the foreshore. It was a glorious autumn morning, with just the right amount of wind and the promise of a spectacular dawn. We pulled on our waders, sprayed the dog, shouldered our guns, and stepped out onto the mud. Or rather Mick did. He was straight up to his knees.

'Not to worry,' he said, calmly. 'There's a technique for this.' He used it, and he was up to his thighs. 'Teething troubles,' he smiled bravely, and was soon in up to his chest.

I was paralytic with laughter, of course, and therefore not much use. But a sudden thought wiped the smile off my face. Mick had checked the tide table that morning. The brown water of the Bristol Channel was due to close over Mick's camouflaged head in half an hour.

I managed to pull him out, leaving those top-of-the-range waders behind. Haste wasn't necessary, in fact. Mick had been reading the tide table for Scarborough. But it was just as well that we got off the marsh when we did. The spray had sent the dog into life-threatening anaphylactic shock. The vet was not amused to be woken at five.

9.

BADSHOT
AND THE
UPPER ECHELONS

MICK WAS VERY EXCITED. He'd been invited to one of the county's best driven pheasant shoots. Way up in the heart of the Blackdown hills, it had everything: high, hard birds; improbably huge bags; the view of the gods towards Exmoor and the Vale of Taunton; a host with immense charm and two brace of dazzling daughters; and the finest lunches west of St James's.

Mick tried to be calm and blasé, but it didn't work. Throughout the summer he'd been surreptitiously reading about the etiquette at flash driven days. I found a list on his desk: 'Pegs numbered right to left,' it read. 'Move up two at a time' And 'Cherry brandy or whisky mac fine in the hip flask: G and T absolutely not.'

One day he made an elaborate excuse to be away for the day. He said he'd been to look at some fencing posts in Exeter, but Jim from our local bumped into him on the train back from Paddington. A few weeks later a large soft parcel arrived with a W1 postmark and the name of a very expensive sporting tailor. Mick, who had taken to rushing to the post every day, didn't get there in time. 'I wonder what this is,' he said, unconvincingly, and crept off to the bathroom with it. The door was loudly bolted, and from inside there was a ripping of wrapping paper.

We were all at the door, of course, eyes applied to cracks and keyholes, and so we saw the beautifully cut shooting suit being worn for the first time. The breeks had a double seat and real silver buckles. The waistcoat cleverly hid the effects of a lifetime of beer and chips, unlike the tartan stockings which clung to his huge calves with the help of those splendid 1920s Cub Scout type garters beloved of the Purdey and Holland and Holland wielders of the Home Counties. He preened himself in there for a good hour, the tweeded peacock, coquettishly trying different angles in the mirror, experimenting with different brogues and watch-chains, and generally making himself very unpopular in a just-breakfasted household with no other bathroom.

On the night before the big day Mick sat up late polishing his shoes, his buckles, and a borrowed English side-by-side with a nice walnut stock and Churchill type game ribs. 'It'll be good to see things done really properly' he said for the thousandth time. 'Quality shows. And that means Old County Quality.'

Strangely, none of the disasters we predicted for him occurred. He got up in time. The car managed to start. He remembered his cartridges. He did up his impeccably tailored flies. He didn't call his host's present wife by the name of the first wife. He didn't tell the one about the nun and the jaffa cake. He didn't shoot any buzzards. He didn't shoot birds that weren't his. In fact he didn't shoot at all. His nerve broke at the end of the long gravel drive leading to the house, and he went and sat mournfully in a lay-by all day doing Sudoku.

10.

BADSHOT'S CHRISTMAS CHEER

'IT'S GOING TO BE THE BEST Christmas ever,' said Mick. 'It's going to be a Christmas with integrity. We will buy nothing. We'll get a proper tree from the wood; we'll hang cartridge cases from it with cord made from pheasant sinew; we've got our own parsnips and potatoes. And the best thing of all,' he continued, as we looked queasily at each other, 'is that the centre-piece of the Christmas lunch will be my matchless Somerset pot.' We brightened up at this, because we knew what he meant. He meant that he would serve up a woodcock inside a mallard inside a Canada goose inside a roe deer. We brightened up not because we were looking forward to eating it, but because we knew that there was not the remotest possibility of Mick shooting any of, let alone all, these things, and that therefore we'd end up buying the turkey that we all really wanted.

But we had misjudged the man. The roe buck was shot in mid-August, on a glorious night when the land was shining and the sycamores were swaying. I was there, and a fine shot it was too: a kneeling shot from 120 yards as the buck was about to disappear into the wood. It was the unluckiest deer on the planet, and although I secretly suspected that Mick hadn't seen it at all and was actually aiming at a squirrel about 90 degrees away, I graciously kept my mouth shut.

His luck outlasted the summer. After his disastrous first outing on the foreshore he rallied, and pumped a couple of thousand cartridges into the early morning sky during September and October. A duck clumsily got in the way of a pellet, the dog, for once, agreed to fetch it, and Mick had his mallard.

But now the contests became laughably unequal. I didn't think there was any point in Mick climbing into the ring against either a goose or a woodcock, and said so. Mick, to his credit, just gave one of those enigmatic Clint Eastwood-type smiles and carried on oiling his gun as if he were in the corner of an Arizona saloon.

The very next morning, out on the Bridgewater mudflats, a small group of Canada geese was grazing just opposite the bank where Mick was holed up. A shot from another distant wildfowler put the group up, but one was left, pathetically trailing a wing. It was plainly an old injury, and it plainly wasn't going to get better. It took Mick several cartridges from almost point-blank range to put the goose out of its misery, but as we drove back home that maddening saloon smile was there again.

The smile started to fade when, in the week before Christmas, there was still no woodcock. We'd asked all the local game dealers to tell us if Mick made any covert approaches to them, but he seemed to be playing straight. I assumed the woodcock had him well beaten. There aren't many woodcock in our woods, and the ones there are aren't obviously brain-damaged or terribly physically disabled. In desperation Mick, with three days to go, made some frantic phone calls and bolted onto a plane bound for the west coast of Ireland. My investigations about what happened there are not complete, but I'm charitably inclined to think that, improbable though it seems, the single woodcock that came back in Mick's hand baggage on Christmas Eve had indeed fallen to his gun. A rapturous beam had replaced the smile. Everything in Mick's world was as good as it could be.

It was a big, family Christmas. We had a house full, and had filled the B and Bs for miles around. I heard Mick rising dutifully early on Christmas morning. I heard him humming 'God rest ye merry gentlemen' as he padded to the game freezer in the garage. And then I heard an unearthly screech; a Hitchcockian wail of angst and woe.

It wasn't Mick's fault that the freezer door had been open for a fortnight. It wasn't his fault that there were no shops open on Christmas morning. It wasn't his fault that the children weren't well bred enough to be impressed by the tiny woodcock that sat in the middle of the table, dwarfed by the piles of tofu that we'd managed to find to go with the roast potatoes.

11.

BADSHOT AND THE WHITE COAT

JUST AFTER CHRISTMAS Mick was gripped by a terrible ennui. He sat in his study, moodily chewing turkey sandwiches and staring out at the flooded fields of the Levels. When the mallard came whirring in he never raised an eyebrow, let alone a 12 bore. When a fox dug in under the electric fence and took a couple of chickens he just stirred on the sofa and said: 'We've just eaten plenty of poultry: why shouldn't he?' This wasn't the Mick I knew: a Mick of demonic and disastrous enthusiasm; of hot and vain declarations of war on marauding foxes. I was worried about him. Stern and immediate action was needed. I picked up the phone and dialled a Fort William number.

I've never seen a man brighten up so fast. 'We're going hind stalking,' I said. And immediately Mick unwound from his armchair, and looked up with a new, predatory sparkle. When I told him that we were catching the train the next day he leapt to the gun cabinet with the agility of a puma. It was an almost Biblical miracle of transformation – as if he'd been told to take up his .270 and walk.

I've always loved that trip up on the sleeper from Euston. The delight starts on the platform as you try to work out who are the real sportsmen amongst the travellers. Sometimes it's easy – a giveaway gun or rod-case, or the sort of heirloom tweed trousers they stopped making in the late 30s. But sometimes it's not so clear, and you have to wait until everyone gets to the bar to pick up the tell-tale scraps of conversation. But there is always – always – someone you know. Or someone who knows someone you know. And so most of the night is spent in happy, self-glorifying reminiscence of Great Shots and Monster Fish. The shots and the fish get longer, and the noses get longer and redder as the night wears on. Then there's bed, somewhere near Carlisle, and then the woozy breakfast at first light somewhere north of Glasgow. Ideally you'll be going to one of the little unmanned stations. If you are, the stalker will pick you up, take you straight away to change, take you for a quick crack at the targets, and with a bit of luck you can be on the hill within the hour. Then London, or whatever else ails you, will dissolve in minutes.

Once you're there, there's nothing like it. Highland stalking would make a poet out of an actuary. Get our sour-faced urban MPs on the top of Torridon with the sun on their backs, the wind right and the clouds streaming in from Ireland, and field sports would be safe. Then, good day or blank day, there's the wood smoke of the lodge fire, the beer in the barrel, the bath, the gargantuan dinner and the ancient malts. It's all wonderful.

These were my fantasies as I leant out of the window of Carriage F at Euston, where I'd agreed to meet Mick. He'd got to London earlier that day, because he'd wanted to buy a special white Norwegian winter combat coat. 'Your green coat in all that snow will send the hinds galloping into the sea,' he'd told me, with his old maniacal gleam.

But I began to worry. Mick was cutting it very fine. The guard walked along the platform slamming the doors. I started to sweat. Where on earth was he? Then, with a huge gulp of relief, I saw him racing down the ramp, portly and puffing, a rifle box in one hand and a vast suitcase in the other. It was all going to be all right. I shouted encouragement. He looked up and waved happily. It must have been at that moment that he slipped. The suitcase burst open: socks, cartridges and a magnificent new winter combat coat spilled out onto the platform. His agonised bellow as the train pulled out of the station sounded like a rutting stag in the echoing glens of north-west Scotland.

12.

BADSHOT, INTERNATIONALIST

'WE'RE ALL MEMBERS of a great international brotherhood,' said Mick, as he ladled a huge spoonful of spinach gnocchi into his furry face. 'The hunting instinct transcends all boundaries of race, colour and creed. We stand shoulder to shoulder with field sportsmen everywhere.' He took a sip of his Bulgarian red, winced, and motioned enviously at my pint. 'You'll have to give that up when they arrive,' he said. 'Ale is an English affectation. It will alienate our friends.'

In an unguarded and slightly drunken moment in the summer, Mick had volunteered to organise a visit to the Levels of a posse of shooters from all over the world. 'It's about time we broadened our horizons,' he said piously. 'We need some new ideas here.' He had become unbearable. He had mothballed his wax-proofed coat, and wore a Loden shooting jacket with silver buttons. He fried his eggs in olive oil. He had given up the ready-rubbed flake he bought from the post office, and smoked some aromatic Italian brand in a Bavarian pipe with a hinged lid and an engraving of a stag kicking a wolfhound in the groin. He had heard that Argentinean duck hunters had perfumed moustaches, so he grew one and doused it with Old Spice aftershave. He had heard that you had to break yourself in gently to the Goat Vindaloo that they ate in Gujarat after a successful hunt, and so added chillis to his corned beef hash and garlic to his ham salad. He learned how to say 'Good shot, my dear friend,' in ten languages, and laboriously unscrewed the toilet seat 'because we don't all do things in quite the same way, you know.' He could convert from rupees to Euros with the diabolical facility of a Kabul heroin trader.

No one could fault his dedication. He drove dutifully all the way to Heathrow to collect a group of Chinese sportsmen, waited there for six hours failing to do the crossword in *TV Quick* magazine, swore only mildly when he found that he'd written their arrival date down wrongly in his diary, and drove dutifully back the next day. He smiled indulgently when the Portuguese contingent turned his Land Rover over in a ditch and made some mind-boggling suggestions to the long-suffering barmaids at The Bell. He spent a good hour in the kitchen laboriously picking lead shot out of an ample set of Albanian buttocks, and even kept his temper when the Spaniards shot a fox and brought it home slung on a pole over their shoulders. His temper was only slightly frayed when he found a Russian, dressed in full commando kit, plus face paint, stalking a sheep in the paddock next door. When some Icelanders threw his Jack Russell into the frozen lake, taking bets (with Mick's AYA side-by-side as the prize), about whether it would hunt Mick's cat (which they had also thrown into the lake), Mick simply tut-tutted and said, between gritted teeth, 'Garcons will be garcons'.

What made him snap was the farewell banquet. It was an elaborate and exotic affair. All the food and all the drink of all the nationalities was exhaustingly represented. Salt cod had been shipped in from Lisbon; gravadlax from Reykjavik; fruit beer from Bruges; black bread from a Ukrainian deli in East London. Pride of place went to the Gujarati goat vindaloo. Mick had palpated every goat under the age of one in the farm next door, and chosen the tenderest, which was a hand-reared favourite called Edith. 'Edith's death is sad,' he told us solemnly, 'but it will cement these relationships, for the good of field sports and so for the good of the world.'

He carried the curry in, beaming. There was an eerie silence amongst the assembled multitude as he placed it on the table, clapped his hands and said, inaccurately, in four languages, 'Dig in, please, gentlemen.'

It wasn't the left-overs that hurt Mick so much. It wasn't even the fact that the room was empty in twenty minutes. It was the cartons from the Taunton McDonald's, clogging all the bins in all the guests' lodgings.

Mick is now an old-fashioned little Englander. He organised a petition to shut down a local Italian restaurant, and won't drink any beer brewed outside Somerset. His accent has got broader and so, from all the steak and kidney pud he eats, has his rump. 'International understanding?' he barks out in The Bell. 'I understand the Internationals all right.' And then he goes back to his thoughts and his ale.

13.

BADSHOT, TARMAC GOURMET

Within the illustration:

SQUIRREL CASSEROLE

ANDOUILLETTE
A303
SPICY ROOK AND PARSLEY

CATS EYE CHOPS
HARE FALLEN A303

WW 07

MICK HAD BEEN GOING THROUGH some rough times. He'd fired off almost a thousand cartridges during the wildfowling season, and his total bag was a flightless mallard that had been paddling sadly round Bridgewater Bay for months, living off bread provided by the local children. 'It shouldn't have been shot,' they said at the bar at the Halfway House: 'It should have been allowed to drift peacefully into eternity in an RSPCA geriatrics ward.' Mick wasn't amused. Nor was he amused in Thetford, where he went to do his Deer Stalking Certificate. He'd confidently identified a sika stag as a baby moose, failed by yards to get his four inch group on the range, yet effortlessly drilled the model of a forester straight through the heart in the safe shooting test.

He was dismayed, too, by the reception of his road-kill recycling initiative. 'It's a scandal,' he told the usual bemused crowd at the Canal Inn: 'Tons of magnificent wild meat are left to rot on our roads every year.' So he toured the lanes of south Somerset with a great vision and a black plastic bin bag, scraping up pheasants, rabbits, a couple of hares, several rooks and a lot else besides. He even had a small badger which he jointed and marinated in cider before the nauseated Mrs Badshot, the most long suffering

were used to the pattern. He holed up in his study, emerging only to eat moodily and to draw circuit diagrams on the edge of the newspaper. Then he was off to the shed. The light went on, the bolt was drawn, and we heard strange bangings and scrapings into the early hours.

In the morning Mick was suavely confident. 'It's going to be a killer,' he assured us. We looked nervously at one another. 'Who's joining me?' he said, making it clear that we had no option. So we all dutifully loaded up and lugged the kit to the best of the pigeon fields. Finding birds to put on the decoy had been an embarrassing problem: Mick had hardly been the Genghis Khan of the pigeon world over the last few months, and we had to buy some from the game dealer.

Mick was at his most maddeningly Napoleonic. 'You over there with the Browning,' he barked. 'You: blacken your face some more.' Mick, intoxicated by tales of moustachioed Victorian earls on huge Norfolk pheasant days having loaded guns handed to them so that they didn't miss a chance, had three guns with him: his old AYA, his Beretta semi-auto and another borrowed semi-auto. 'I've only eight shots before reloading,' he said, doubtfully. 'I hope it'll be enough.'

When we were all in place, Mick placed the pigeons tantalisingly on the machine, connected up the motor to the battery, said 'here we go,' and flicked the switch.

The motor whirred into life and the spokes began to turn. We were impressed. But after a few moments it seemed that something was wrong. Instead of turning in a leisurely circle the spokes gathered colossal speed. They turned like the rotor of a massive and powerful helicopter. The pigeons at the end were a grey blur. And then they came adrift. One flew off and hit Mick squarely in the chest, knocking him to the ground with a strangled scream. The others sailed gracefully into the field. One went a good hundred yards, and must hold the world record for the longest flight by a dead bird.

Mick picked himself up, muttering about the need for a slight readjustment. But sadly he had left the battery and the switch underneath the now lethal rotor. He couldn't get anywhere near it. There was nothing for it but to leave the machine running until the battery ran down. That still hadn't happened by the time dark fell, and so Mick left it overnight.

I wonder if the fox that gnawed through the cable got a nasty shock. Mick certainly hoped so. Or perhaps the machine had already been ruined by then by the badgers that rolled on it. We shall never know. And Mick declares that he doesn't care. 'Real sportsmen,' he told us loudly in the Halfway House the following week, 'don't need any help from technology.'

16.

BADSHOT AND THE ANIMAL ANALYST

MICK'S SOMERSET VILLAGE HAD SEEN SOME CHANGES. To his disgust it had lost the shop, the post office, the bus service, the pub and the farm workers. But it wasn't all loss. It had gained a mobile phone mast (stuck on the church tower to finance the roof repairs), several e-businesses, a suspension tank in which you floated in order to remember what it was like in the womb, an aromatherapy clinic, and a great wave of stressed refugees from city life who lived on organic yoghurt and the interest from their redundancy pay-outs. Mick saw himself as the leader of the resistance against these 'in-comers', as he called them. His resistance consisted of muttering darkly in the Halfway House about 'the rape of the land', although he was never able to say exactly how the flotation tank violated anybody.

One bright Spring morning he was out in the fields behind his house taking some absurdly optimistic shots at some completely safe pigeons. He had his dog with him, and when all the pigeons were feeding provocatively just out of range, he took out the dummy launcher and tried a few retrieves. This was always good exercise for Mick, because the dog just sat looking mildly interested at Mick's waving and whistling, and remained sitting happily while Mick bounded off into the undergrowth and returned bearing the dummy. Mick wasn't a bad retriever at all, and the dog always welcomed him back with approving tail-wags.

Mick had just emerged from a bush, and was trotting back to the dog, when a high pitched Californian voice screeched out: 'You have a real problem there, my friend. And so has your dog.' Mick looked up in astonishment. Striding towards him in a kaftan and steel toe-capped work boots was an extraordinary woman. Her hair was green, and tied up in a teetering, vertiginous bun. Her face was deeply lined and strangely hyper-mobile. One set of false eyelashes had come adrift in the wild wind of the Levels, and swung across her eye. In one hand was a lead which led, so Mick assured us, to a white rabbit in a harness. In the other was a small cigar which she alternately pulled on and jabbed towards Mick's face to make points as she spoke.

This, Mick realised, was Angeline D. Fleisch, PhD, who had just bought a house vacated by the blacksmith (who had moved to Swindon to work for an insurance company). She, the gossip went, was an Animal Psychoanalyst and a Pet Bereavement Counsellor. Mick

had seen a new sign on the Parish noticeboard which said (inside a rainbow border), that Dr Fleisch could help if your dog was having a turbulent puberty, if your cat was dangerously jealous, or if you yourself couldn't come to terms with the loss of your tortoise. He had seen her car parked in the square at Ilminster: a mucus-coloured Robin Reliant van with stickers across the back window saying 'Dogs are deep', 'Ants have angst' and 'Probe-a-Pet-a-Day'.

She dived into her cleavage, plucked out a business card, tucked it into Mick's cartridge belt and said: 'I will see you both this afternoon at four. Dress casually and bring a photograph of your mother.' She flung her cigar down, ground it under her heel, and marched off towards the church, where she was running a jam stall. Mick was incapable of speech. He took out the card, read it carefully, and set off home looking thoughtful.

Well, he went at four, we later discovered. We could get no details from him, but happily client confidentiality isn't a crucial principle in the world of Cognitive Bestio-Therapy, as it's said to be called. For the price of a pint of farm cider, Dr Fleisch was happy to tell all. 'It was a barn door case of role reversal,' she said, helping herself to a fistful of pork scratchings. 'The dog wanted to be a dog, but Mick wouldn't let him. Mick was being the dog. That creates all sorts of weird psychological nastinesses. So all I did was to chain Mick inside a kennel, bark at him and feed him a bowl of dog biscuits. After an hour he swore he'd never retrieve again. He also swore.'

Mick wasn't available for comment, but Dr. Fleisch became our friend that night. She turned out to be an enthusiastic and expert wildfowler, and saw no conflict with her work. She drank her cider and belched: 'A dead duck has nothing at all to worry about – that's how I see it'.

17.

BADSHOT
AND THE RIGHT AND LEFT

AS USUAL, as the sun began to sink into the Levels, Mick Badshot whistled up his hopeless dog, shouldered his AYA, and strode off up the lane. Soon he was at it. We always knew when it was Mick shooting. There were always two shots in rapid succession, followed by the distant noise of cursing echoing through the elms. He never hit anything on the first shot. And he never hit anything on the second either.

Tonight, though, when he came in as empty-handed as ever, he wasn't taking any of the usual jokes. He was in a foul mood. He had walked into the *Halfway House* the night before and had sat quietly in a dark corner, nursing his pint of cider and beaming out at the world. Then in came Mervyn and Eddie. They bought their beer and sat down near Mick , without seeing him. Mick was just getting up to join them when he heard his name mentioned. He sat down again and listened.

'We've had some UN inspectors in our village,' Mervyn was saying. 'They came to look for some weapons of mass non-destruction. They took all Mick's guns for analysis.'

Eddie guffawed and sprayed a passing barmaid with Otter Ale.

'And they do say,' Mervyn went on, that the local rabbits queue up to get right in front of Mick's gun. Safest place in Somerset.'

Eddie choked on a piece of pork pie.

Mick, wounded deeply ('Unlike anything he fires at,' Mervyn would have said), crept out of the pub, sat mournfully in the Land Rover for a while, and drove slowly home, a plan hatching in his head. 'I'll show them,' he said to us. 'A fully witnessed right and left will shut them up.'

And he tried. How he tried. I had to go with him whenever he went up to the wood, but so far as I could see, Mervyn had been completely right. Mick ran accidentally over a hedgehog on the way to Langport one night, but apart from that the wildlife of the Levels was safe from him.

Gradually the wounds began to heal. Mick began to grunt at Mervyn again; and then to speak to him. Winter turned to spring, and spring turned to summer, and Mick began to think about things other than the shame of the *Halfway House*. In particular his badly twisted mind started to turn to the village fete.

This was the usual thing; a collection of stalls selling Victoria sponge and unwanted

THWACK
THE
RAT!
£1 a go: a packet
of polos if you hit the
rat 3 times.

copies of Barbara Cartland and *Knave* magazine, an opportunity to sling wet sponges at the deeply disliked curate and, year in, year out, Mick's commercially catastrophic 'Thwack the Rat'. Readers will know about 'Thwack the Rat'. It involves putting a stuffed sock into the top of a sloping bit of drainpipe, and then trying to hit it with a baseball bat or other club when it emerges at the other end. It's surprisingly hard. Everybody in the village knew that it was hard, and so found Mick's offer ('£1 a go: a packet of Polos if you hit the rat three times') easy to resist.

So Mick stood, unpatronised as usual, fuming at the lack of initiative of the younger generation (in whom he included everyone who hadn't fought at Agincourt), and watching resentfully the money changing hands at the 'Stick the tail on Posh Spice' enterprise run by the local plumber, whom he despised.

As he did every year, Mick was just about to stalk off, never to return, when the vicar and his wife arrived, sipping weak tea from old china cups. Mick had a soft spot for the vicar. He was a gentle, lisping soul, keen on steam trains and the old Prayer Book, and had done time in his youth for importing a massive consignment of cannabis resin.

'Oh, well done, Michael,' said the vicar. 'Good show. Now just remind me how it's done.'

Mick was only too delighted.

'If you'd just put the rat in the top, Your Holiness', he said, with a wink to the vicar's wife, who thought that the parishioners took her husband too seriously. 'I'll deliver the coup de grace to the iniquitous rodent.'

In my mind's eye the next few seconds are in slow motion. First I see the vicar delicately putting the rat in the top of the tube, and Mick twirling the bat professionally in his hands, like a Redsox pro. And then I see Mick's upstroke catch the vicar elegantly in the point of the chin, and the vicar hurling up his hands and screeching, and falling to the ground in a crash of shattered willow-pattern. And then I see Mick's epic down-stroke, and the rat emerging unscathed, and the bat landing with colossal force on Mick's sandaled foot. And then I hear Mick's gargantuan bellow which makes the icing on the fairy cakes tremble. And then I hear Mervyn snigger quietly: 'Ah, Mick. So you got your right and left after all.'

18.

BADSHOT AND THE NEW TECHNOLOGY

'THIS IS AN AMAZING DEVICE,' enthused the salesman, sweating in his polyester suit at one of the few country fairs that had survived the monsoonal summer. 'It can detect your ferret through 20 feet of rock. And just look at that digital display. It shows exactly how far away you are.' But Mick, predictably, was not impressed. 'What's wrong with instinct, young man?' he snorted. 'Whatever happened to the *art* of field sports? Whatever happened to that mystical link between a ferreter and his ferret?' He stalked off to look at a scary display of burst gun barrels, shouting over his shoulder, as a parting shot; 'And do the Sioux of the Minnesota woodlands need a liquid crystal display to lead them to the White-Tailed Deer?' But the salesman back at the stand was busy making a digital display which involved no technology at all.

I reminded Mick of this conversation when, a couple of nights later, just as dusk was falling, he lay with his ear pressed to the grass above a big warren in the field by the pigeon-flighting wood, straining to hear the sound of his favourite jill in the bowels of the earth. He looked viciously round at me before using the same ancient symbol that the salesman had used. We heard later that the jill had been found by an interior designer, visiting the village from London. He had dyed the jill pink to match his carpet, and it lived in a silver box in his Fulham flat. That didn't improve Mick's mood.

Mick does learn from his mistakes. But unfortunately he doesn't always learn the right thing.

'There's a place for technology,' he told us one dinner-time, as he gnawed on a rabbit thigh (bought in Waitrose, of course). 'But here's the principle: always use the lowest possible level of technology.' We waited with poised forks, too anxious to eat the next mouthful. We knew that something else was coming, and we knew it was likely to end in tears. 'I've solved the ferret problem,' said Mick, looking gratified at our expectancy. 'We simply combine two disciplines: fishing and ferreting. We use my double-handed salmon rod and attach a strong line to the ferret's collar. If the ferret gets stuck, we simply reel in.' We sat amazed. Mick saw our amazement. 'Yes,' he said. 'It's brilliant, isn't it?' 'But…', we all started. 'But why didn't you think of it?' broke in Mick. 'Because your minds are too cluttered with technology to think of beautifully simple solutions, that's why. Never mind.' We looked at each other ominously, resigned to another catastrophe.

It was one of those glorious gloaming nights in the Levels. A roe buck picked its way delicately through the deep undergrowth in the wood by the farm, and Mick's pointless winter flight pond was alive with dragonflies. Mick had picked a splendid warren to try out his new scheme. There were at least thirty holes in a bank beneath some tall, whispering elms. He took out his oldest hob, tied some stout nylon line to its collar, and let it go. The line whirred smoothly off the reel as the ferret went into the tunnels. Soon a couple of fat rabbits were struggling in the purse nets. The ferret emerged from a hole on the other side of the warren, but that was no problem. Mick just untied it, put it in its box, and reeled the line in. The problem we'd anticipated – the line getting snagged and tethering the ferret underground – didn't happen. Mick was buoyant and smug. And his smugness grew and grew as the evening wore on. The old tawny owl flapped silently across the field. We began to shiver, and said it was time to go. 'Just one more time', said Mick, who was having the time of his life.

So out came Doris, a scarred old jill, veteran of many a fight and many a confrontation with foxes (because to Mick, a hole's a hole). And in she went, mustard keen. There was a mighty thumping below, but no rabbit hit the nets. We waited. And we waited. The owl came back, carrying a vole. 'Edna is having her tea down there,' said Mick, and no doubt he was right. So he picked up the rod and began to reel in. It worked wonderfully. The ferret was plainly being hauled smoothly back. Mick beamed and reeled and looked at us for approval, which we grudgingly gave. And then the reeling stopped. Just visible, but well out of reach, the ferret had got wedged sideways on across the tunnel. However much slack Mick gave her, she wouldn't struggle free. 'There's nothing for it,' said Mick. 'You'll see now how good my system is.' So he planted his feet against the bank and heaved. The rod bent with the strain.

I'd never appreciated before just how powerful a good salmon rod is. Nor had Mick appreciated the need to put the ratchet on the reel. We saw a magnificent thing. Against that sunset we saw Edna flying across the wood, narrowly missing the first pipistrelle of the evening and lodging, mewing piteously, in the top of one of the old elms, hanging safely but uncomfortably from a tangle of nylon line.

It was the strangest call the Taunton firebrigade had ever had, and the end of Mick's contempt for liquid crystal displays.

19.

BADSHOT AND THE SHOT PATTERN

THROUGHOUT THE LONG, lush days of summer, Mick Badshot had leant on the bar at the Halfway House drinking cider and telling his glazed-eyed listeners about his preparations for the coming season. 'I missed a couple of long shots last February,' he said. 'I think that I'll shoot with two-thirds choke on the right barrel and half choke on the left. Those woodcock won't know what's hit them.' And indeed he did fiddle around with his chokes. And his ammunition, his stock lengths, his barrel lengths and his boots. He even changed his brand of oil, saying that when he was shooting hard and fast at high geese the heat caused his old brand to evaporate. 'The greylags can smell two parts in a billion, you know,' he droned with Papal authority. 'It makes the next wave veer away.' I will never forget his self-righteous sneer when the barmaid (who'd shot a pigeon or two in her time), said that that might have more to do with the noise of the first fusillade. 'Er, no,' he assured us. 'It's the polycyclic hydrocarbons binding on the same receptors that the geese use to track down their favourite grass types.'

Now the nights had drawn in, the guns had been drawn out and Mick's season had begun. It hadn't been blessed with the murderous success he'd predicted. Indeed the only certain casualties were a rabbit with myxomatosis that fell to the ninth shot at point-blank range, and a cartridge bag he'd left in the gents. It was all the fault of the chokes, of course. 'I just wonder if Geoffrey Boothroyd was right about half choke for those really tricky low shots on snipe in bad light,' said he. And we, exchanging tired glances over our pints, didn't have the heart to say that it was nothing to do with chokes: that a child's catapult or a long stick would have done better.

Nor, I'm afraid, did we have the heart to invent other engagements when he looked soulfully at us over the pork madras and asked, 'Will you help me fine-tune things?' We should have known better.

It started well enough. When we got to his house we found evidence of surprising professionalism. He had rigged up some big paper screens on wooden frames at carefully measured distances from the firing point. On the screens he had painted some huge, crude pheasants and some genetically modified rabbits. The idea was to fire at these figures and decide, having looked at the pattern, how the chokes should be tweaked.

We set up the thirty yard screen, and Mick went solemnly to the firing point, raised the

gun and fired. He put the gun down and trotted earnestly to the screen. We watched him peering at the paper and scratching his head. We went to have a look. The enormous deformed rabbit was completely untouched. Mick sat down on a log, took out a notebook, did some calculations of apparently Einsteinian complexity, and then took up his gun. He did something earnest with a screwdriver, re-loaded with a determined click, and fired again. The rabbit was unscathed, but Mick's pride was not. 'I knew it,' he blustered. 'I knew it. That gun's hopeless. It's going in the bin.' He handed the gun to Ernie. 'Shoot me,' he said calmly. 'I'm going to go down to the eighty yard mark. You fire straight at my backside. I'll be perfectly safe.' Ernie, being a sensible, law-abiding bloke with no criminal record, refused; and so did we all. And so it was that Angus was fetched. Angus, the toast of Her Majesty's prisons from Inverness to Truro, picked up the gun, aimed it at the distant Mick with a confidence born of a life-time of building society robberies, and pulled the trigger.

It took several hours to pick the shot out of Mick's buttocks (the most repellent job the local vet had ever done, he said), but much less than that for Mick to devise the explanation. It was an aberrant shot weight, apparently.

20.

BADSHOT DOES HIS BIT FOR ENGLAND

MARTIN WAS A GERMAN DOCTOR with a passion for field sports, a shooting lodge in a forest near Berlin, and the bad luck to sit beside Mick Badshot at a wedding. Absurd though he is to those who know him, Mick has a superficial plausibility. Through four courses and the speeches we listened to Mick's tales of effortlessly long shots at twisting woodcock, heart shots from the hip at charging buffalo and the five greylag he took with a single rifle bullet: 'I'd run out of shotgun cartridges, so I took out the .243, waited until the geese were in a line, and drilled them all with one shot.' We looked at each other and sighed. Martin was agape, and we knew that there would be trouble. There was. Martin was scribbling his details on the back of the menu: 'It will be a pleasure and a privilege to host a sportsman of your calibre. We cannot hope to offer you sport of the quality you are used to, but we will do our humble best.' Mick shrugged modestly, and before the bouquet was thrown (and caught by Mick's male black lab – 'Always knew there was something funny about him,' said Mick), they had fixed dates in December for some driven wild boar. I knew a bit about this sport, and thought that Mick's chances of survival were remote.

Mick applied himself to his preparation with his usual demonic energy and consummate lack of judgment. He spent hours finding out which brand of gun oil worked best at low temperatures. 'The central European winter is so cold that the pheasants can't fly. They're just like iced aeroplanes. Their wing contours are changed by the ice, and they have no lift. You can walk around and club them with your gun butt.' We listened obediently. 'Your feet often freeze to the ground,' he went on. 'You have to learn to fire behind you without being able to move your feet.' He demonstrated this in the field behind the house, and the insurers subsequently refused to pay for the window, the willow pattern tea-set, the framed photo of Mick being gored at Pamplona, and the crate of corn plasters that he'd bought at auction thinking they were chocolate digestives. Then he changed tack, and started researching the best brand of gun oil for high temperatures. 'We'll be firing off forty rounds a minute', he said. 'Our barrels will be glowing red. And the schnapps they ply you with makes you shine like a Belisha beacon.' We all breathed a huge sigh of relief when he went off to Stansted for his flight.

I supposed we shouldn't have expected him to have sorted out the permits for his guns, but somehow we did. Mervyn wasn't amused to have to drive out to the airport to pick them up. Mick was unabashed and unapologetic. 'It's a good thing, really. Local firearms are always the best. I could only ever trust a Mannlicher in those woods.'

He was back two days later, pale, silent and limping. Over several months and from several sources we pieced together what happened in Germany.

Mick was full of largesse and supremely confident inaccuracy. He carried it off well, we heard. When someone, the night before the drive, had tentatively questioned whether he was right to say that Burchell's zebra raised their calcium levels by eating lion cubs, he grandly and graciously waved a hand and said: 'Not any more in the main commercial hunting areas, of course. Quite right. You have to get off the beaten track by a couple of months to see it these days.'

Mick had been given the best possible position on the drive. On either side of him were some young but experienced Austrians, utterly in awe of the sporting god they understood they had in their midst.

When the first boar came through, Mick was transfixed. His rifle fell to the floor, and he watched in amazement as the boar came past. The Austrians, thinking that the Great Man had seen some subtle but compelling reason not to shoot, held fire too. This happened twice more, the Austrians still respectfully silent. But then they decided that they couldn't miss out completely on their day. The next wave brought three splendid boar racing straight for Mick. The Austrians opened fire. These things can be pretty scary, but there was no need for Mick to hurl himself to the ground screaming 'I'll go quietly. I never meant it.' We never did discover what he didn't mean, because by the time a magnificent, prize-winning Weimaraner had closed its teeth in the part of his left buttock spared by the Pamplona bulls and his own shot-pattern test, he had quite forgotten. Apparently Air Berlin have quite soft seats, but you can't mop blood off them with those little packs of wet wipes.

21.

BADSHOT
AND THE BIG
FREEZE

IT WAS BITTER. The wind that brought snow to the Levels also brought redwings, fieldfares, general malaise and a minor pile-up on the A303. It was said that a heron on Sedgemoor had dozed off with its legs in the water and had been trapped when the pool iced over. Myth grows quickly in this part of the country when there's nothing else to do: they said that the crescent-shaped marks made on the ice as the heron flapped and floundered meant that planning permission would be given for a mosque in Taunton. No one ventured out. The hunt met in the town square on Boxing Day, drank the cooking sherry resentfully given by the new non-hunting landlord of the pub, (who'd been told he'd lose business if he didn't carry on his predecessor's tradition), and trotted home after a token half hour in an icy field.

Mick Badshot, pickling walnuts in the kitchen, was scathing. 'We're a pitiful, namby-pamby nation,' he said, between mouthfuls of mulled cider. 'Jack Mytton' (he'd got a biography of the mad Shropshire hunting squire for Christmas) 'would sometimes be so excited by the chase that he'd strip completely naked and ride in the vanguard all day, until there was no skin left on his buttocks. Do we see that sort of commitment amongst modern sportsman? I think not.' 'Do we want it?' ventured the incautious Mrs Badshot. 'Indeed we do, Mrs Badshot, indeed we do', said Mick, who had just seen *Pride and Prejudice* on the TV, and thought that this was probably how Jack Mytton would have spoken to his brutalised wives. 'Jack Mytton ordered his servants out on ice skates to hunt rats on frozen lakes,' Mick went on, 'and drank eight bottles of port a day, just to wash his brandy down with.' 'And died at 38 in a debtors' prison,' rejoined Mrs Badshot. 'Is that another reason to admire him?' Mick went sullenly back to his pickling, muttering about sucking the marrow out of life. But Mrs Badshot's blood was up, and she could see her quarry failing. 'And while we're at it,' she said, her hands now on her hips in the traditional position for wives taking the moral high ground, 'the woods haven't seen much of you since it got a bit chilly.' Mick coloured, and then pickled silently in an agitated way, like a heron trying to get out of a frozen mere.

Very early the next morning we were woken by Mick. Loudly and unnecessarily he told us that he was off to do a bit of shooting. He didn't need company. 'It'll be too cold for you,' he insisted. 'I'll see you later.' He made a point of showing us that he was hatless and gloveless and wearing a thin cotton shirt and shoes. Mrs Badshot was worried. 'Now don't be silly,' she said. 'You'll catch your death.' 'Why's that, Mrs Badshot?', said Mick. 'It's positively summery out there.' He lifted a shivering hand to us as he strode out into the snow, which was peppered with starlings, dead from the cold.

He was gone for many hours. Every once in a while one of us would hoist himself up from a fireside armchair and look out into the white void, or check the modern thinking about the treatment of frostbite ready for Mick's return. But Mick wasn't frostbitten. He came jovially in, stamping the snow off those inadequate shoes. 'A good day,' he said. 'Plenty of really difficult woodcock and the odd pheasant. But I didn't have the heart to shoot them – not with the weather making their lives hard enough as it is. It was just a pleasure to be out.' We stared at him, and stared at the clock. He'd been out for a good five hours, and all his fingers were still there. 'I think I'll crack open that bottle of Cockburn's. But maybe a brandy first.' We watched as he poured himself a glass, raised it to the fox mask over the mantelpiece, and drank 'To the Winter Wonderland.'

Snow is a revealing thing. There were no footprints going up to the wood or into the fields. There was one set. It went straight from the front door to the garden shed. And there, alongside the sleeping bag that Mick had been lying in, and the fan heater he'd had on all day, was the biography of Jack Mytton.

22.

BADSHOT GOES BEAGLING

EARLY IN THE NEW YEAR Mick Badshot looked in a mirror. He was horrified at what he saw. 'I was a nymph,' he said, 'and the mince pies have made me into a gigantic Caliban.' Then he got breathless running after a traffic warden in Taunton, looked in his *Readers' Digest Home Doctor,* and was afraid. 'I'm teetering on the edge of eternity,' he said. 'I have looked obscene obesity in the face: now I am looking at death itself. Cheers.' And he finished his pint and ordered another.

But in that laborious Jurassic way of his he had learned a lesson. Next day he rang up the Master of the local beagles. 'I'm at your service,' he said. 'Well, thank you,' said the Master, doubtfully. 'My ferrets,' said Mick, 'produce the most aromatic urine in Somerset.' 'Right,' said the Master, presuming that Mick was yet another tragic victim of Class A drugs. 'And your hounds will love it,' Mick concluded triumphantly. The penny dropped. Mick was offering to mark the trail demanded by the ridiculous Hunting Act, with which our beagles are of course strenuously compliant.

Hunting these days is rightly concerned about its image. It wants to appear friendly and inclusive. Our Master runs his hunt like a church youth club. Everybody is needed, everybody is wanted, and nobody ever does anything wrong. There are no orders; there are just gentle suggestions. It is disastrous. 'That would be great, Mr Badshot,' said the kindly Master, and far off I seemed to hear demons cackling.

Mick got himself impressively into trim. He ripped the seats of two pairs of tweed trousers trying to touch his long-invisible toes, and ripped the gusset of another doing an arabesque over a barbed wire fence. He sprinkled bran on his coco-pops and drank cod-liver oil from a pewter tankard. He carefully removed the dark chocolate truffles from the huge tin, and gave the rest to the dog, who threw up in Mrs Badshot's hyacinths. He bought a medicine ball and hurt his foot trying to kick it over the rugby posts at the local school. But at last he proclaimed himself fit.

We never did discover how he managed to extract the ferret urine, but there were some strange whimperings, crashes and shouts in the early hours from the shed where the ferrets were kept, and one morning Mick, three fingers heavily bandaged and his nose bleeding, held up a small bottle of musky liquid. 'This'll send them wild.' He was right.

The day of the meet was dull, grey and drizzling. At the pub, bemused Australian barmaids handed round sausage rolls, farmers muttered that the end of the world was nigh, and a little knot of surly anarchists in nylon anoraks scowled from under their hoods and plotted with OS maps how they were going to ruin everyone's afternoon. 'Look at them,' spluttered Mick. 'Since when have they cared for the rule of law?' He struck a blow for freedom by telling the Australians that if they gave the antis any sausage rolls he'd get their work permits revoked.

The line Mick laid was, for a while, a great success. His ambitious plan (to have the hounds hunt a trail that spelled out 'Bollocks to Blair') was thwarted by an impenetrable withy bed that Mick hadn't known about, but it was good nonetheless. But then it all went terribly wrong.

He had made up a thin porridge of ferret pee and rabbit stock, and was carrying it in a plastic bag. Clambering through a hedge, Mick stuck his foot under a root and fell with a curse and a splendid, balletic twist. He fell right on top of the bag, which ruptured. Mick was drenched, but, all credit to him, he kept his head. He knew what was coming. His wrenched ankle meant that he couldn't walk, but he hopped across the field, and when he fell again he crawled fast.

It was a magnificent, elemental sight. He went for four fields on his hands and knees before the hounds caught him, and when they did there was pandemonium. It looked like a huge shoal of Great White sharks in a feeding frenzy. The whippers-in needed a lot of help to pull hounds off, but that might have been because they were paralytic with laughter. It was all captured on video by the antis, and an outraged article later appeared in an underground broadsheet in Bristol, denouncing hunting's appalling inhumanity to man.

Mick, for once, would have agreed with the antis. 'A very dangerous occupation, hunting,' he said, having come straight back to the Halfway House from the Accident and Emergency Department with a diagnosis of twisted ankle and shock-induced palpitations. 'Not at all good for your health. Cheers.'

23.

BADSHOT MAKES A FRESH START

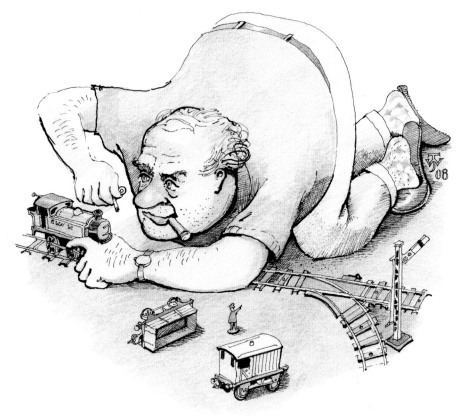

THE EARLY BUDS OF SPRING and of Mick Badshot's rekindled appetite for field sports were beginning to peep up. The winter had been a traumatic one for him – full of humiliation, disappointment, cancellation and personal injury. His grandiose schemes had been sniggered at in the Halfway House; his dogs had got kennel cough; the only pheasant he accounted for all winter turned out to be a beloved, tame, hand-reared one called Susan. His love of shooting wavered and finally hibernated. His guns sat in the cabinet, well-oiled and unused. Occasionally he would take one of them out and sit by the stove, turning the gun over on his knees, stroking it and recalling entirely fictional long shots and big bags. And then he would replace it with a sigh and go back to his model steam railway. When he retailed his unbelievable yarns to long-suffering bar maids it was with the airy detachment of a retired grandee: 'When I used to shoot,' he would begin, as we all winced, gulping cider to numb the pain of the next hour of monologue. Under the influence of that cider Mick's rabbits became elephants, his sticklebacks barracuda, and his .410s punt guns.

The dying flames of the pub's beech wood fire consumed the last remnants of Mick's credibility and the last vestiges of politeness on the part of his audience. 'No you didn't,' the fightback would begin. 'I was there, and you missed with five shots by about half a mile. It was too lame to move, which is why you elected to shoot at it in the first place, and Mervyn had to walk over and knock it on the head.' Mick always tried to preserve his dignity. 'No, no, dear boy,' he would murmur, graciously, 'I remember the time you are talking about. But of course I was shooting humanely at a colony of disabled shrews in the same field as that rabbit. I don't suppose you saw them.' But even Mick knew, eventually, when he was beaten. 'Very well,' he would say, sadly. 'I can see when I'm not wanted.' 'No, no,' we would all chorus, but it was no good. He would slope mournfully home.

For Mick, public reminiscence was almost everything, and if he wasn't to be allowed that, he could see little point in maintaining his shotgun licence. 'I'm fed up with this game,' he said, and bought a new consignment of signals, buffers and grassy knolls for the railway. But as the main game seasons ended and the sun returned to the land, his interest re-awoke. 'It won't be long,' he mused, before the young rabbits are sunning themselves on the bank by the wood. And soon I'll be able to have a serious go at those magpies in the name of conservation, and the tench will start to move in the Parrett'. He looked up with a bushy-tailed resolve. 'And I, I will be there waiting for them all.'

Just as everyone else's were put away, Mick's guns were taken out, polished until they dazzled in the thin rays of that mean March sun, and fired earnestly at the safest tin cans in the West Country. The deadly dangerous home-loading factory was re-opened in the shed, the coat was re-waxed, the dogs were wormed and made to practise their water-retrieves, the boots were re-soled and the sporting spirit generally buffed up and refurbished.

On a glorious, windy March day, when the hares were dancing in the field behind the farm and we were frantically checking the phone number of the local Casualty department in anticipation of the inevitable disaster, Mick was ready to re-launch himself into the world of field sports. He strode cheerfully out, full of hope and bacon and eggs, the huge legacy of a winter's inactivity straining a waistcoat to tensions undreamt of by the Harris weaver. He had his favourite AYA side-by-side under his arm, a pocket full of his own cartridges, and a touchingly optimistic game bag over his shoulder.

He was away for quite a while. We heard shots up at the wood and wondered what impressive lies would be told to explain the empty bag. About four o'clock, in Mick wandered, ruddy-faced and beaming. He put his gun on the table, and silently took out of the bag five splendid wood pigeons and a couple of perfectly respectable rabbits. We stood agape, and we remain agape to this day. They were apparently genuine. We have no evidence at all to suggest otherwise, apart from the laws of probability and the fact that Mick had never previously been known to hit anything that he was aiming at. But on that magnificent spring day the gods had welcomed the prodigal back. This was an ordinary, decent, successful shooting day, which is so utterly remarkable for Mick Badshot that it deserves a book all of its own.

BADSHOT AND THE RURAL RENAISSANCE

'SOME OF THE OLD COUNTRY CRAFTS have revived, it's true,' said Mick, with the high-priestly tone he always uses when he's about to leap onto a badly lame hobby horse, 'but what about the arts? Where are the poets and the writers? Where are the artists and the sculptors? Where are the Landseers, the Munnings, the Snaffles, the Edwards and the BBs?' I wearily slung him a magazine, and told him to glance at the classifieds, but he wasn't going to have his speech spoiled by the facts. 'We need a new rural Renaissance' he went on, the light of insanity flashing brightly through his bifocals. 'It will begin here, in south Somerset. Ilminster will be its Florence. And I will be its Michelangelo.'

This came as a surprise even to those of us who have known for decades Mick's capacity for self-delusion, suffered for it and tried to mitigate its excesses. Mick has many qualities, but artistic genius is not prominent amongst them. If you want an account of the history of muzzle-loading, an emphatic and wildly inaccurate summary of the pros and cons of gin traps and snares, or a list of the Masters of the Taunton Vale between the wars, he's your man. But if you want a recognisable sketch of a partridge, you'd be better off asking the cat. Compassionate, mild-mannered Julian at the Halfway House put this as kindly to Mick as it could be put. Mick was unabashed. 'The Muses visit those who ask, dear boy,' he said, and started on his second lamb korma of the evening.

So the shed became 'the studio', his moods became 'the agonies of creative childbirth', he smelt strongly of white spirit, and his best trousers were stiff with burnt ochre. Every Monday night he went off to still life classes in Taunton: 'Not *life* classes, you understand,' he hastily reassured us. 'That's for the deviants. Mrs Badshot wouldn't like that at all, and the central heating in that church hall isn't good enough for it to be humane.' Instead of taking his gun up to the wood, he staggered up the lane with an ostentatious easel and daubed happily away for hours, coming back to tell us about the 'luminous quality of the light' and 'the intimate communion of the painter and the ageless land'. We asked if we could see his paintings, which always produced a quiet smile and a wave that he plainly thought was Parisian. 'All in good time. I understand your excitement, and it's very flattering of you. Good things come to those who wait. Leonardo couldn't stand being watched at work, and never showed his work until the moment was perfect for its consummation.'

We didn't have to wait long, in fact. The following week ragged handwritten notices appeared on parish noticeboards and telegraph poles across the region. 'Mick Badshot, Sporting Artist and Rural Philosopher, requests the pleasure of your company at a private view in Isle Abbots Village Hall. Paintings, sketches and sculptures all for sale. Prices from £50.'

The attendance at Mick's events is generally bad or non-existent, but not so with this one. When the day of Revelation dawned, a crowd of sceptical farmers, cider-makers, plumbers, cocaine-dealers and merchant bankers, representing the whole rural community, clustered in the drizzle outside the hall. Mick swept in, late and unapologetic, wearing an absurd tweed smock and a beret. 'Can you see the hunger in the masses?' he breathed. 'Centuries of soul starvation. We will feed them.'

He did. He fed them with memories they would never forget. They filed obediently into the hall, took the cups of Fanta from the trays, and started to look around. There they saw, hanging on the walls and standing on the trestle tables, the most horrible things. Children screamed and ran to their mothers; the cocaine-dealers blanched; the plumbers winced. Terribly deformed plasticine horses straddled fences; crude and monstrous birds leered from branches; packs of the sort of dogs you stop drawing when you go to nursery school ran through green-strip landscapes with blue-strip skies. Legend says that the suns had smiley faces, but that presumably isn't true. The farmers and cider-makers drank up their Fanta and bolted queasily for the door. The brave ones sniggered.

'This is amazing,' said a smart-suited man who had just moved into the village from London. 'You have an astonishing, iconoclastic talent. Can you come to Town next week to meet a friend of mine?' 'Indeed I can,' said Mick, beaming. And now he exhibits in one of Mayfair's best galleries, has appeared on a mid-week chat show on Radio 4 and is booked to give a lunchtime lecture at Tate Modern. You'll not get the smallest Badshot for less than £5000, and he'll never have to work again.

25.

BADSHOT GOES RATTING

THE RATS OF SOUTH SOMERSET were on the move. Nobody understood quite why. It wasn't that the weather had been particularly warm, or the cats particularly idle. But they were everywhere: in every drain, every barn and every shed. They were big and confident, and of course they got bigger with every pint. 'Like coypus, they were,' said Mervyn, at half past seven in the Halfway House. 'Arrogant, shaggy and completely amphibious.' By ten o'clock they were 'more like brown, yellow-fanged badgers, with scaly tails the size of an adder.'

The bar became like Monty's ops room as the counter-attack was planned. Maps were laid out; the merits of poison, traps, gas, guns and dogs were earnestly mooted. The most surprising people showed astonishing technical knowledge. A barmaid known previously for other attributes turned out to have a PhD in biochemistry and the cunning of a serial killer. A relief milker had been fired by Rentokil for sleeping in his van, but had learned a lot when he was awake. The mild-mannered youth from the saddlers who had previously only been animated when talking about hoof-oil could apparently shoot a .22 rifle from the hip.

It brought out the best in dogs, too. An ornamental poodle from Fivehead, universally despised, soon had hundreds of rat scalps to his credit, and minced round the lanes with a new pride. Snuggles, a Pomeranian from Curry Mallet, was re-named Attila by the admiring populace after a long and testing afternoon in a ditch.

Ratting isn't my idea of a good day out, to be honest, but the rats engendered a community spirit not seen since the war. That's because it *was* war. It was a war, though, in which everyone came out to watch. 'Going ratting this morning?' the milkman would ask, and the answer would generally be yes. Phones buzzed as intelligence about the latest infestation was passed around. Someone suggested that the times and dates of the ratting meets were posted on the Village Hall website. If the weather was good, the turnouts were immense. TVs were switched off, illness feigned, and cakes made. The spectators sat cheerfully on the grass or on the deck chairs they had brought with them, gambling away their Income Support, passing round egg and cress sandwiches, and discussing the conformation of the dogs like pundits at an Ascot collecting ring.

Mick Badshot looked on, stroked his many chins, and wondered.

'It's all very well,' he said eventually. 'But nobody's doing this properly. This should be a chance to recruit the next generation for field sports.' We all pointed out that the ratting seemed to be achieving precisely that, but he wouldn't have it. 'No,' he insisted, 'it all needs to be more organised. We must have the biggest and best ratting party of all. While enthusiasm is at its height, I will explain that what they are enjoying is not just fruit cake and country sport, but the taste of fundamental freedom – freedom denied to many English sportsmen; freedom being daily eroded by the oppressive State. Then I will pass round petitions and Countryside Alliance membership forms. We will reclaim south Somerset for St George.' We sighed, as we had sighed so many times before.

But it all looked auspicious. In the week of Mick's 'Say Rats to the Hunting Ban' session (as he had called it, against all advice), there were more rats than ever. Every pipe seemed to have a quivering nose in it.

Mick had decided that the epic event should take place in his barn. He had laid out seats in layered rows, so that everyone would have a good and comfortable view. A tea urn steamed on a trestle table, next to barrels of cider and ale and plates of pies and buns. A cup bristled with pens that the multitudes would use to sign all the paperwork. Mick's own dog, a black lab called Ziggy, had been denied her breakfast so that she'd be keen.

All the punters filed enthusiastically in, filled their plates, and sat down. The local dogs eyed one another like boxers before a bout, knowing that honour was at stake.

'Right,' said Mick. 'We're ready. Stand back.' And with a pitchfork he started to move the bales where, he assured us, rats were swarming. But there was nothing. Absolutely nothing. 'They'll have gone a bit deeper,' said Mick. 'They'll have been alarmed by the noise.' So he dug deeper, and still there was nothing, and we could all see the sweat on Mick's neck and the rising colour in his face. And then, at last, there was something. A house mouse ran out. Disoriented by the crowd, it made straight for Ziggy, who whimpered and raced out of the barn with her tail between her legs. Mick followed.

There were no rats that day, but there were many subscriptions to the Countryside Alliance. 'Best afternoon I can remember,' said the postman. 'If you can get so much fun from seeing an animal being chased, hunting's a wonderful thing.'

26.

BADSHOT
AND THE HIGH SEAT

SOMERSET SLOSHED AROUND IN MONSOONAL RAIN. Cars floated, demure high streets became rivers of mud, sullen London journalists in inadequate coats and designer wellies clogged the trains from Paddington, and Mick Badshot paddled his homemade coracle down his drive and all the way to the goat farm for his milk. The big rabbit colony in the red earth bank by Mick's stretch of the Yeo was washed out: the quick ones migrated up to the pigeon wood; the slow ones were washed downstream and eaten by the already swollen rats or disgorged into the estuary. Meadows dry for decades became marshes; hard-pressed farmers with suffocatingly small margins sought refuge from rain and depression in the Halfway House, muttering that it was a vintage year for liver fluke, and that'd be the final nail in the coffin of south-western agriculture.

And then, as suddenly as the water came, it went. The farmers found something else to be depressed about, and Mick took to walking for his milk again. The journalists, having drained Taunton of latte, headed back east in the hope of an assignment in Tuscany, and the rabbits moved back to their old quarters in the bank. Mick was glad about all of these things. He didn't know enough about liver fluke to feel confident about shooting his mouth off, and was relieved he could get back to the defects of the CAP, which he had diligently studied and which had won him many a pint over the years. The coracle had turned over in full view of a party of young offenders doing their community service, with predictable results in terms of hilarity, loss of dignity, and damage to a new suit. And the rabbits' return to the bank was just as well, since Mick's great spring project had been to build a hide in a tree overlooking the bank.

Mick's girth had expanded massively over the winter. It meant that he really couldn't stalk rabbits by crawling up to them, as he used to say he used to do. He was so fat now that if he lay on his front he rolled either forward (with his face in the field), or backwards (so that he couldn't get his elbows to the ground). Neither position was great for aiming a .22 rifle. In the occasional moments of uneasy equilibrium his backside was so far off the ground that even the partially sighted wildlife of Somerset stared in wonder. So he had decided to 'go continental', as he ludicrously put it, shooting (or at least shooting at) rabbits from a high seat, as one might shoot roe deer or wild boar.

The seat was made of green oak with swirling Celtic designs carved clumsily into it to satisfy Mick's New Age leanings. It was pegged elaborately to the trunk of the host tree with wooden pins of the sort that Mick said had been used for the hold of *The Victory*, it had a beautiful wooden roof that channeled rain cleverly into a butt at the foot of the tree, and you got into it by climbing an elegant ladder with ingenious handrails made from copper piping. There was plenty of room for the two comfortable arm chairs that Mick hoisted up there, cup holders for the brew, and the whole thing was swathed in the best quality camouflage netting that the British Army had ever sold off dirt cheap. As high seats go it was the bees' knees. It was lovingly and thoughtfully designed, with appropriate deference to traditional methods and ecological principles. It was a splendid place to spend a sporting evening. In fact there was only one thing wrong with it. It was impossible to fire a single shot from it into anything other than the branches of the tree.

A massive unloppable trunk stood directly between the high seat and the rabbit bank. By hanging onto a branch with one hand and swinging dangerously out to one side it was just possible, in the leafless depths of winter, to see one unoccupied hole.

Mick, of course, maintained stoutly that it was all intentional. 'That hole,' he said, 'belongs to a massive buck rabbit with clairvoyant senses. He's the sort of rabbit of whom myths are made. I've been hunting him for years. There's a strange bond between us. This is the only way that anyone could possibly get him.'

'Yeah, right,' said the irreverent barmaid at the Halfway House, who didn't understand the deep mysteries of the sporting life.

27.

BADSHOT, NATURE'S FRIEND

SPRING AND EARLY SUMMER had seen a huge and deadly outpouring of conservationism from Mick Badshot. He had heard that drowning was a major cause of death in barn owls, and had crept out at night and put grates over the cattle drinking troughs in all the neighbouring fields. 'Cows have long, almost prehensile tongues,' he assured us. 'They'll easily be able to lap what they need through the bars.' The cattle, desperately dehydrated, had broken down three fences and an ancient, ecologically significant hedge to get to the river. The farmers threatened legal action.

Mick then wanted to encourage swallows. He made some nests from modeling clay, baked them in the oven, and stuck them with araldite under the eaves. The swallows seemed wholly uninterested. Mick told the unimpressed barmaids at the Halfway House that this meant that this year's swallows had come from northern Mozambique. 'The nests there are more conical, of course. I'd assumed that this year's, like all previous years', would have come from the central Congo, and I designed the sort of nests attractive to Congolese swallows.' It was only after all the local swallows had hatched their eggs that Mick realised that he had left no entry holes in his nests. Then one of the nests fell off, lightly injuring a visiting clergyman and providing a convoluted sermon illustration for several south Somerset Sundays.

The garage was full of cardboard boxes, each of which housed an emaciated and doomed young bird, 'rescued' by Mick from its happy but slightly clumsy life as a fledgling. Mick was devoted to these birds. He got up early every morning to do the rounds of the boxes, giving a different, exotic and immensely improbable cause of death to each of the corpses. One night the cat got into the garage and did swiftly the job which Mick's misguided mercy usually took several days to do.

Then there was the grassland management project. 'It's vital,' said Mick, over the fourth pint of Roger Wilkins' magnificent cider, 'that we encourage the old, native species of meadow plant. They're the ones that all our animal species evolved alongside; they're the ones our wildlife is really at home with. We've got to have bottom-up conservation. Get the fields right and everything else will come tumbling after. And I,' (he tapped his nose knowingly and, because of the cider, rather inaccurately) 'know how to do it.'

It turned out that he had made a concoction out of beer, arrowroot, turpentine and 'several secret ingredients'. 'The native plants love this stuff,' said Mick. 'They thrive on it. But the invaders can't bear it. In a couple of weeks we'll have the sort of meadow that we haven't seen in this country since the Middle Ages. And then, very quickly, the land will come alive again. Long-embattled insects will suddenly find a niche; hedgehogs will be eating for the first time in centuries what they were designed to eat, instead of toxic imports; we'll see just how big the slugs of Old England were, and the beetles will shimmer with the forgotten colours that inspired the shields of the Crusaders.' 'Right,' said one barmaid. 'Nice,' said another.

If Mick was right, mediaeval England must have been like the central Sahara. He sprayed his mixture over all his own fields, over one of the fields of the only farmer who had forgiven him for the water troughs, and over Mervyn's rockery. The effect was dramatic. Within a day everything was yellow and wilting. Within a couple of days everything was obviously dead, and Mick himself was seriously endangered. He was being hunted by Mervyn, armed with a baseball bat, and the farmer's solicitor, armed with a slimline briefcase containing a summons to the local County Court.

28.

BADSHOT ARRIVES,
BUT DOESN'T

A LETTER FROM LONDON fell onto the black labrador that was sleeping on the doormat in Mick Badshot's Somerset house. Stumbling downstairs after a hard night at the Halfway House's goat-racing competition, Mick picked the letter up, peered at the post mark, and went to his study. He came out with his favourite letter knife – a bayonet rumoured to have been the nemesis of fourteen Germans on the Ypres salient. Its next victim was Mick's thumb. When he had mopped the blood from the lino, and tied an insanitary rag round his hand, he opened the letter with his second-best paper-knife (made from a muntjac's ear: a road casualty, of course; Mick had never knowingly got within half a mile of a muntjac when armed in a way permitted by the Deer Act.)

Mick's screech of delight was louder even than the screech that had delighted us when the bayonet burrowed into his hand. It drowned even the squeal of the dog as Mick trod on it en route to the kitchen to tell us about the letter.

'I've arrived,' bellowed Mick. 'Recognition at last.' And it seemed that he was right. By an administrative error which was subsequently the subject of a searching internal inquiry, Mick had been invited to the *Shooting Times* drinks party at the CLA Game Fair.

His preparations filled the next month. A new tweed suit was ordered from Jermyn Street, rejected in favour of lederhosen with a silver stag head badge over the crotch, and then restored. Anxious consideration was given to the old Loden hat with its jay's feather, but it finally gave way to a supposedly jaunty Panama, anointed (according to the dishonest auctioneer who had seen Mick coming from miles off) with the blood of a Colombian jaguar.

The shoes were discussed for weeks. 'It has to be the Veldtschoen boots I was wearing when I shot the Namibian wildebeest,' said Mick, at first. 'They have real authority.' But he began to have doubts. 'Perhaps those fell boots that they all wear in the beer tent at the Rydal Show. Or the Trickers brogues that saved me from a broken foot when that gelding stood on me at Chatsworth. Or perhaps the suede shoes that danced The Dashing White

Sergeant so nimbly in the lodge at Conaglen.' We wearily endorsed each suggestion as it came, hoping it would be the last.

On the night before the Game Fair it was all decided: it would be a white linen suit, the fraudulently stained Panama, some two-tone golfing shoes and a perpetually glowing Montecristo.

Mick's research had been impeccable. He had written out on little cards the names of the *Shooting Times* staff and their regular writers, and had tapped the wells of London and Somerset gossip for details of their backgrounds. He had well-rehearsed and cleverly personalised opening lines for any and all of them, and had sketched out detailed plans for the subsequent conversations. He reckoned that the editor had a soft spot for Spanish partridge shooting, and had memorised the menus at the main sporting hotels so that he could entrance with local colour. For Lawrence Catlow he had at his fingertips the very latest research on lice in sea trout. And so on and so on.

Nothing had been left to chance. His ticket had been booked weeks in advance on the internet. The recommended AA route to Blenheim was hanging neatly from a clip on the dashboard. Even the Land Rover had been serviced.

It was therefore a surprise when Mick took the wrong exit off the M4 and found himself wholly disorientated in some very beautiful Wiltshire countryside. But a phone call convinced him that the universe was still on his side. Some of his mates were in stationary traffic between Oxford and Woodstock, having taken two and a half hours to travel six miles. As the tales of woe on the approach to the Game Fair multiplied, Mick felt happier and happier. 'We'll have a proper lunch in this excellent pub,' he said, 'and then ease up once the traffic's subsided. It'll give me a hour to go over my cards again.'

And that's what we did, and excellent it was too – a real Pickwickian feast of steak and kidney pie, treacle tart and several pints of local beer. It was so good, in fact, that there was no possibility of Mick driving on, but that was no problem: thinking prophetically that something like this was bound to happen, I'd been on the orange juice.

The problem was different: the newly serviced and superbly performing Land Rover was evidently performing superbly for some joy-riding youths miles away.

There was no taxi to be had for love nor money. Hitching is hard at the best of times, but it is probably particularly hard for a middle aged man in a white suit and golfing shoes, visibly drunk and carrying a shotgun over his shoulder. In any event it didn't work for Mick. At 6.30 pm, when the worthies of the field sports world began to file into the *Shooting Times* enclosure, Mick was sitting slumped in a lay-by, glumly answering the questions of the earnest young policeman who was excited to be involved in his first armed incident.

29.

BADSHOT AND THE CIDER PRESS

DESPITE A LIFETIME OF DISAPPOINTMENT, ridicule and serious personal injury, Mick Badshot continues to be a gullible romantic. If someone tells him that the Cavaliers shot their black-powder charges down barrels thinner than modern copper tubing he'll be down to the plumbers' merchant, into his workshop and in the ambulance on the way to the Accident and Emergency Department quicker than you can say 'Er, only joking.' After he heard that the druids treated burns by immersing the affected part in boiling hemlock he had to sell his car to pay for the plastic surgery. He was once arrested for stalking the geese in St James's Park with a bow and arrow after a radical misreading of some ancient documents convinced him that an edict of 1397 entitled all yeomen resident in SW1 to 'take by bow, snare or howsoever all waterfowl there situate'. He still believes that the reason for his eventual conviction was that the magistrates were not convinced that staying in an SW1 hotel on a three-day Beer n' Bingo Special counted as residence within the meaning of the document. In fact it was because the 'edict' was a fiction made up by his Romanian tour guide, who wisely failed to appear at court.

So it was alarming when Mick, in the grip of one of his periodic obsessions with rural authenticity, decided that he was going to make his own cider. Equipped only with limitless enthusiasm, a skin impervious to criticism and a print-out from Wikipedia, he set to work.

First he built himself a press from long screws (provided on request by a well-known local handler of stolen goods) and pieces of plywood. Then he bought some barrels (previously used for paraffin) from a garage, and a second-hand dog bath.

Then there was the matter of the apples. It was only late in the day that he realised they were necessary. He had had visions of traditional cider apples from orchards going back to the Domesday Book: apples with evocative names like Broxwood Foxwhelp, Breakwell's Seedling, Sheep's Nose, Yarlington Mill, Stoke Red, Brown Snout and Stembridge Cluster. But even in south Somerset the Chancellor's evil tax on native antiquity had bitten hard, and for a while it looked as if he might have to make do with Spanish Golden Non-Delicious from Asda. But finally he ran some of the real apples to ground in a forgotten orchard near the Devon border – an orchard guarded by the happiest apple-fed pigs in the kingdom and a fierce matron called Helga with a chin as bristly as a badger's bottom and a pending Crown Court trial for shooting a trespasser.

We spent a deeply unhappy day in that beautiful place. Mick, inevitably, was treed by the pigs, who knocked his ladder down as he reached for the topmost apples, and when he came down he was knocked over and snuffled almost to unconsciousness. But at last the harvest was gathered in, loaded into the back of the Land Rover, and taken back home.

All the household blenders in South Somerset were borrowed, plugged into a massive battery of extension leads which fused the system twice, and into them the apples were fed. The result was a dog's bath full of pulp, and a huge sense of foreboding.

A great multitude assembled to help with the pressing. Coats were removed, biceps were flexed, reputations were staked. At which point another crucial omission was noted. Mick insisted on doing things properly, and that meant that the juice had to be filtered through straw.

'No problem,' said Mervyn. 'Back in a minute.' And he was, wheeling a huge barrow full of straw.

So Mick proudly built his 'cheese' – alternating layers of apple pulp and surprisingly aromatic straw, and the horny-handed sons of agricultural toil who inhabit Mick's village (most of whom have degrees in accountancy or fortunes made in the derivatives markets) took their turn on the press. So the juice flowed, Mick beamed, and a TV crew making a film about the life of Thomas Hardy panned around and drank the cooking sherry.

The juice was barrelled up, blessed by the local vicar, and consigned to the garage. And there it stayed in the oily dark, gaining gravity, gravitas and complexity.

Just before it was due to be tasted, a nasty rumour began to circulate about Mervyn's straw. It was never very precise, but it involved its earlier use for the bedding of some calves that had had the most spectacular rotavirus diarrhoea the vet had ever seen. He'd even written a paper on it for the *Veterinary Record*. Mervyn made no admissions until a heavy night in the Halfway House, on the very eve of the unbarrelling. Yes, it was true, he said. He'd thought it would be amusing, and had intended to tell everyone as soon as the pressing was complete, but then had seen Mick's happy face, and couldn't bring himself to ruin it all.

He needn't have worried. That cider was the best anyone had ever tasted.

30.

BADSHOT AND THE LURE OF THE EAST

MICK HAD GONE UP TO LONDON to stay in a well-known West End club to which he had been unaccountably elected. There is presumably another Michael Badshot of stupendous accomplishment and erudition who sits mystified at home, wondering why his application was rejected. Mick padded round the Club library, asking the baffled librarian (formerly of Trinity College, Cambridge), if the latest Andy McNab book had come in, and shattered the monastic calm of the dining room by calling loudly for brown sauce with his sole.

As he always does, he wandered round the gunmakers, sporting tailors, vintners and cigar merchants, peering hungrily through the windows, picking up guns whose case he'd have to remortgage his house to buy, squeezing into jackets meant for lithe dukes, squeezing and sniffing Havanas with a bogus authority that fooled nobody, and asking disgusted Masters of Wine if they could recommend a decent rosé for less than four quid a bottle.

And as he always does, he went back to Somerset from Paddington station. Things happen to Mick at Paddington. Bad things. He was arrested there once for absent-mindedly pocketing a piece of prune crumble, twice somersaulted down the steps of the gents, and regularly boards slow, stopping trains to Oxford when he's trying to get to Taunton.

This time, though, it was all different. He left himself plenty of time, and went through into the arcade at the back of the station, where he found the splendid Japanese restaurant. He sat down on a stool and for twenty baffled minutes watched the circling conveyor belt bearing all the dishes before he worked out, with the help of a cosmopolitan plumber from St Ives, what was going on. Then there was no stopping him. He ate his way through everything on the belt, and staggered onto the last train to Taunton heavy, happy and with a new vision for money-making.

'Our native rivers,' he boomed in the Halfway House the following night, 'are heaving with the most tremendous resources. And do we exploit them properly?' He looked round, expecting fascinated rapture, and, because he's tragically deluded, seeing it where there was in fact bored resignation. 'We do not,' he continued, banging the table for emphasis. 'The Japanese: they know how to do things properly. Sushi: that's the way forward. Simple, almost fat free, and wonderful. Our own Somerset waters are alive with sushi.' The terrifying truth dawned on the few drinkers who hadn't crept off to watch paint dry. He was going to catch carp, tench, eels and chub, hack them all up and try to persuade people to eat them raw with seaweed from Bridgewater Bay.

And that's what he did. For a frantic fortnight he feverishly fished the Levels. He lay under a road bridge near Langport for a night, having been told that there were monster carp in a deep pool there. (There weren't.) He ground-baited a mill-pond near Fivehead for a week, hoping that the epic eels written about in the mediaeval parish records would creep out from the tree roots. (They didn't.) But he did reel in a fair number of diseased roach and some seriously brain-damaged perch, and they swam around in an improvised tank in the garage, awaiting execution.

Mick had announced in the local paper and on the parish notice board that 'Somerset Sushi: full of Western Promise: Motto: We do our best to plaice,' would open for business that Saturday. He had been interviewed on local radio by a bemused journalist more used to car boot sales and phone-ins about cystitis. He'd even had a couple of threatening phone calls from animal rights activists. It all looked very promising. Outside the house he put up a board covered in oriental writing copied from an in-flight magazine (noted by Lt. Colonel Briggs, known for his derring-do in the Korean campaign, to be an advert for a Seoul escort agency). Mick sat in the garage, knife in hand, plates and seaweed piled up beside him, happily disemboweling and slicing up the slowest of the roach. He'd been down to the bank that afternoon, and had £400 in loose change – 'because sushi eaters tend to pay with twenties and fifties'.

'They'll be here soon,' he said, half an hour in. 'Not long now,' he said, after an hour. 'It always takes a while to get a new business going,' he said in hour three. The only customers were cats, in their dozens. The garage undulated with them. But it may have picked up. Sadly we will never know, for in his frustration Mick sliced the roach slightly too aggressively, dividing his superficial digital flexor tendon. When he was released from hospital five days later, the cats had had all the remaining fish.

31.

BADSHOT AND THE SCOTCH MIST

'YOU'LL HAVE TO JOIN US IN PERTHSHIRE,' gushed the colossal woman, before collapsing into a rubber plant. And Mick, his British reserve elbowed out by the thought of a day on the moor, had the effrontery to write to her the following week, saying that he'd really enjoyed meeting her at the Dog-B'Reath's garden party in Ilminster, hoped that the Casualty Department at Taunton had treated her well, that the scarring wouldn't show, and that he'd be delighted to accept her kind invitation to shoot grouse.

Perthshire was silent. 'They'll be on the yacht at Monte Carlo,' Mick assured us all. 'She really took a shine to me, did Lady Prudence. Said I had the bearing of a well-bred Weimeraner her father had run over with his Bentley.'

He waited another fortnight, reading about ticks, heather burning and butt design, and then, cursing the Post Office, re-sent his letter. Each day he trotted vainly out to meet the postman, but the reading continued and the fantasies grew. Eventually he picked up the phone, and with a persistence honed by decades of being fobbed off by bank managers, managed to hack his way telephonically through jungles of protective butlers, housekeepers and secretaries to Lady Prudence herself. Mick put on the speakerphone and beckoned us all round.

'No, we don't want any life insurance,' boomed Lady Prudence. 'But if you keep on pestering my staff, you'd better sell some to yourself.'

Mick flushed the colour of Lady Prudence's nose, but he rose magnificently to the occasion.

'Lady Prudence,' he purred. 'Lady Prudence. Mick Badshot here. I do hope my letters reached you, but in this degenerate post-colonial world, I very much doubt it. I've rung to enquire after your and your dogs' health.'

It was wondrous to behold. In a minute the old dragon (known in Scotland for having a brooch made out of a ghillie's ear) was eating out of his hand, laughing girlishly at his sycophancies and telling him coquettishly how the tweed knickers of her youth had made her inner thighs numb.

And so he was invited for a day's shooting in the company of some defrocked peers with ancient names and huge hipflasks, some fresh-faced wannabe Parliamentarians ('Very strategic,' whispered Lady Prudence. 'Catch 'em young: Make 'em obliged') and some Russian mafia billionaires who arrived by helicopter, wore combat kit and proposed, until a tactful Tory suggested otherwise, to mow down the grouse with their AK47s.

'It was all wonderful,' Mick told us later. 'A splendid example of how field sports bring together people of goodwill from all cultures. By the time the port went round we were all brothers.' Yes, he said, there had been a spot of nocturnal nastiness when one of the Russians, equipped with infra-red night vision equipment, was caught in the early hours by the butler in the shrubbery outside the au pair's bedroom. The ensuing scuffle had landed the Russian through a plate glass window, and the butler in the local Job Centre. 'Boys will be boys,' laughed Mick, with his infuriating man-of-the-world tolerance.

The shooting, said Mick, was the stuff of the most fantastical sporting dreams. The birds came fast and furious, in wave after wave, more like huge squadrons of modern fighter planes than anything biological. The butts were at a perfect height for Mick, and each had a little stone shelf on which was a small but perfectly formed decanter of old island malt. Mick had gone up with his two best guns, but had been told on arrival that two would be hopelessly inadequate. He'd been lent a third – a Holland and Holland whose trigger guard was worth more than the GDP of Burkina Faso – 'and did I need it? Indeed I did. I fired as fast as I could. My trigger finger was blistered. All the safety catches on that estate are disabled: the Head Keeper says that if you've a gun in your hand which you don't need to fire within seconds, he's not earned his wage.'

'The scale of the slaughter,' said Mick, philosophically, back home in the Halfway House, 'was frankly a bit much for me. I like to see big bags, don't get me wrong. But there are limits.' He drank his cider and shook his head, as if to exorcise the legions of resentful ghostly grouse

It was Mervyn, with his nasty suspicious mind, who thought to check with the estate. An impenetrable fog had come down that day, the keeper complained. There had been no shooting at all.

32.

BADSHOT GOES FOXING

THE NIGHTS DREW IN, and Mick Badshot drew in too. Before the clocks changed, he had been in the habit of wandering round the hedgerows with his gun and his hopeless dog, or sitting in the pigeon wood and firing vainly into the treetops before returning home for his sun-downer, the Archers, and the expected but always absent adulation of the long-suffering, hard-bitten and hard-biting Mrs Badshot.

But as the sun left the fields, and better men licked their lips and oiled their safety catches in anticipation of big pheasant days, all the sun left Mick too. He retired to his library, his whisky and soda in hand and his spaniel-headed pipe clenched in his yellowing teeth. And there he'd sit in his old club armchair, staring into the coals, throwing the occasional slipper for the dog to retrieve (the only successful retrieving it ever did), and occasionally hoisting himself onto his hind legs to pull down a book from a shelf. He'd shift moodily into the dining room for his supper, where he'd bark and grunt. He'd only eat game ('This is a sporting house, you know') which drove Mrs Badshot to distraction, and very nearly to divorce or homicide. Mick's married and biological life dangled on a very fine thread when, firing off a fusillade of racist clichés, he scraped her bouillabaisse into the bin. 'I wish you'd just get out of the house,' she screamed. 'You think of yourself as a hunter-gatherer. Go and hunt and gather.' We gasped and held our breath. Although we all thought it, no one had ever said it to Mick's flushed and pocked face. Mick rose silently, his dignity intact but his flies undone, and stalked off into the study.

It might all have blown over had the local fox not chosen that night to kill all the chickens in the pen outside. 'Not only do you not provide,' wailed Mrs Badshot as she picked up the corpses. 'You can't even stop the fox providing for himself. What's the point of a pair of guns if they're beaten every time by a set of teeth?'

That went home, and hurt. Mick winced. If he'd had a tail (and there was a faction in the Halfway House that suggested loudly that he had), he'd have tucked it firmly between his ample thighs as he crept off to lick his wounds.

We heard him pacing and cursing all afternoon behind the locked door of his study. At teatime he slunk into the kitchen, smelling of smoke and Laphroaig, to dispense some strained bonhomie and eat a bucket of custard creams.

'That fox,' he announced. 'That fox is an ex-fox. It is no more. The curtain is about to descend on its little drama.' We smelt danger, even through the whisky. 'But this time we'll do it properly. None of your namby-pamby halogen lamps mounted on the back of a Japanese 4 x 4. Not for me. We'll do it like they did it in the Neolithic. All predators are drawn – up to a point – to fire. They'll come to the edge of the firelight and stand there, mesmerised. Fortunately for me, and unfortunately for them, that point is well within the range of a well-aimed spear.'

We assumed he didn't mean it. Even by the supreme standards of insanity that Mick Badshot had set, this was beyond the pale. We stood, fascinated and horrified, as he whittled a snooker cue to a deadly point using his (hopefully purchased but tragically unused) skinning knife, pulled a blazing brand out of the fire, and marched out into the night.

All sorts of questions sprang to mind. Was it legal to spear a fox on a Sunday? Would his BASC insurance cover him for this expedition? Were we under some sort of obligation to report a maniac? Would he remember to change out of his carpet slippers?

We only ever discovered the answer to one of those questions. In the porch, Mick held his flaming torch just a little bit too high, and the newly tarred roof caught beautifully. It was a splendid sight. We were lucky to catch it early, and only the porch was wrecked. BASC didn't pay, and quite right too. Mrs Badshot took an extra job to pay for the repairs, and the hunter-gatherer went back to his armchair ruminations.

33.

BADSHOT IS LEVELLED IN THE LEVELS

'OH DEAR,' SHOUTED MICK, or words to that effect. And I could see his point. A great cloud of wood pigeons had drifted slowly just above his head. There really were a lot of them. The fields for miles around were plunged into darkness as they flew over. This were not a flight, but a feather blanket. They made a bee-line for the wet rhododendrons where Mick had crouched for hours, looked down his gun barrels with supercilious assurance of complete safety, landed in the tree just behind him to emphasise their knowledge of his inadequacy, and then flew off, bored, when they heard his fourth impotent shot.

Coming out of the rhododendrons, Mick fired a petulant broadside at a tree where, a long time ago, an extended family of pigeons had been, and tripped over a root.

It was a lot easier to get the mud out of his gun barrel than it was to fix the tibial fracture, but six months later, with more steel in him than a battleship, Mick picked up his gun and limped again towards the wood. The orthopaedic surgeons at Taunton were very impressed with him. Never, said the Consultant, had a man put on so much weight in so short a time. Mick was vast. He didn't look like a land mammal. He should have been a plankton feeder. But he was even more smug than he was obese. He had read everything there was to read about shooting. He was full of ballistics. His table talk was of trajectories and shot weights and foot pounds. He had an absurd little laptop which he had programmed to calculate the lead time which he would have to give to a moderately nourished late autumn teal coming in from the right out of low cloud. On chokes he was encyclopaedically dull. But he had only fired a gun once in those six months, and that was clamped in a vice in the toolshed, fired at a board to check the pattern.

Shooting for him was war. The pigeons had done his leg in, and laughed as they had done it, and he was out for revenge. His was a high-tech war. It made Desert Storm look like a spat between toddlers.

But walking wasn't easy with a bulk like his. He took his gleaming gun psychopathically out of the slip and waddled up the lane towards the first gate. 'This is it,' he said to me. 'This is my pay-back for those months of pain. They won't know what's hit them.' Then he opened the gate.

The ambulance came surprisingly quickly. It was probably only a ruptured ligament, said the paramedic, but with a weight that large it might well be a badly ruptured one. Mick was very brave. He said nothing on the way to the casualty department apart from some muttering about a flight of pigeons which had swooped low over him when he was lying on his back by the gate.

34.

BADSHOT, BUSHMAN

AS THE RAIN SWEPT ACROSS THE LEVELS from the angry Bristol Channel, and the frost burned the last of the colour from the land, Mick Badshot's thoughts, fuelled by frustration, farm cider and manic re-readings of *Jock of the Bushveld*, turned south. In his study, lined with books about derring-do in hot places, Mick thought of zebra and lion. In his icy bedroom, watched glassily by Victorian hunting trophies bought at secondhand shops, he dreamt of record-shattering kudu. In the evenings he dressed in a thin white jacket and went shivering to the Halfway House to ask, in an affected colonial accent, for his 'sundowner' – though the sun had long since left Somerset for happier places.

One night he arrived there with a packet of malaria pills sticking showily out of his jacket pocket. 'Didn't realise that mosquitoes could survive this cold weather,' said the irreverent barmaid. 'They can't', barked Mick. 'I'm off to Namibia'. And he was.

The very next day Mick and his .308 went off in a cab to Heathrow. 'He'll be back later tonight,' we all said. He'd had ambitions like this before, but he'd always failed to sort out the paperwork for the rifle, sprained an ankle slipping in the Gents at the bus station, or come down with some exotic pox allegedly contracted at the travel clinic. On the last occasion he'd been arrested when he'd opened up his sandwich box at Gatwick to offer a flapjack to the armed policeman, seeing him as a fellow sportsman in need of succour. Out from the box had poured five rounds – not of ham sandwiches, but of live ammunition. Mick, spread-eagled on the floor, making the day of that poor, bored bobby, had uttered some trenchant and legally inaccurate words about basic liberties. He escaped in possession of his Firearms Certificate (although not his self-esteem), which shows that there is a God.

So we waited schadenfreudically in the Halfway House, our phones on (although of course on silent, because it's that sort of pub), looking forward to hearing about the latest catastrophe, and speculating loudly about what sort of disaster it would be. The canny money was on one of the offences under the anti-terrorism legislation, but there was a potent and persuasive faction contending for some sort of minor sexual misunderstanding involving a domestic animal. But the phones didn't blink all night.

Mick had flown suavely and efficiently to Johannesburg. There he had overnighted in a pre-booked hotel, eaten Springbok steaks and flirted with the receptionist, and tripped off the next morning, refreshed, shaved, highly scented and self-satisfied, to catch his plane to Windhoek. His hosts had met him at the airport, driven him to a beauty spot, plied him with gin and tonic as blesbok and hartebeest lolloped past, and then driven him to the camp. There, after a deep bath and zebra-striped towels, he'd gone into a superlative dinner. The dining room had looked out over bush as near-virginal as Africa has to offer. Cicadas whirred, hyenas laughed, corks popped, and all was right with the world. After dinner, Mick, resplendent in his new safari suit, and a glass of ancient malt in his hand, bent over the maps of the reserve. 'I bet the wildebeest love it there in April,' he'd said. And: 'A nasty ravine for puff-adders, I'll be bound.' His hosts, astonished that there was anyone prepared to pay the outrageous prices of their first, wildly optimistic estimate, had nodded sycophantically.

At last it was time to break up the party. 'We've an early morning and a strenuous day ahead,' said the newly enriched host. 'Straight after breakfast we'll go out to the range, check that you can place a decent group, and then get hunting.'

We know now what Mick's response to this apocalyptic announcement was, but nobody guessed it at the time. We know now that he blanched inwardly, squirmed, and knew that there was no chance of an adequate group. But he is a man, and he nodded, half-saluted, and bid them a slightly slurred goodnight.

In the morning he was gone, leaving a message saying that he'd been called away to urgent business in Cape Town. The local taxi had been summoned in the early hours. The tan that he said was due to a day lying in wait for a leopard was found to be due to a week on a beach on the Cape. And how do we know? We know because a ritual de-bagging in the Halfway House car park showed a sunburn pattern on his lower body much more consistent with a flimsy thong (later discovered hidden in his sock drawer) than with the thick trousers, scagged with acacia thorn and specked with blood, that he swore he'd worn throughout the trip.

35.

BADSHOT AND THE WINTER WONDERLAND

SNOW, FORECAST FOR MONTHS, fell in tons, to the apparent bafflement of England. The country stopped. Tube trains stood idle, for some reason that no one could explain. Brave would-be commuters shivered under rugs in their cars, listening to gloomy weather bulletins and infuriatingly cheerful DJs and waiting for roads to be gritted with grit that apparently didn't exist. Phone calls to every business in the land were met by voicemail messages or the single strained, sullen secretary who had the misfortune to live close enough to walk to work. The Government, unwisely, praised the efforts of everyone who was keeping the infrastructure working, while everyone else laughed cold, hollow laughs, and noted that the infrastructure wasn't working at all.

Only children and Mick Badshot loved it. Mick's cheerfulness lost him his few remaining friends. No one was in the mood for pious lectures about how it was good for us to know that we couldn't control everything; that we were pawns in the hands of the weather gods. No one wanted to be told how innocent childhood pleasures were the best, and if we couldn't enjoy playing snowballs, we had lost our souls. And so Mick sat on his own in the Halfway House, a pint of cider at his elbow and snow on his boots, wrapped in fur and self-righteousness.

And then, to Mick's delight, someone came in whom he'd never seen before: a newcomer to the Levels and to the pub. A young lad from the city, dreamily enamoured of Somerset, full of Thomas Hardy and bucolic romance, carrying a *Farmers' Weekly* that he didn't understand, and dangerously desperate to learn. Mick pounced like a starving fox on a pheasant poult. He bought the lad a drink, fed him pickled eggs, wassailing legends, fake folk tales and tall stories about greengages, and invited him to come tracking.

'In weather like this,' said Mick, 'the countryside is a book to me'. He recovered himself. 'Even more of a book to me than usual, that is.' The boy stared at him with blasphemous reverence. All his fantasies had come true.

The boy was putty in Mick's hands. They met the following morning, and set off across Mervyn's fields.

'Now there, m'boy,' said Mick, pointing to some scratches in the snow made by Mervyn's terrier, 'we have the last stand of a leveret against a large adult stoat. A male leveret, I think, slightly lame in the off hind, which is doubtless why it met its death. And the stoat was the third largest of the second litter from behind the old tree, from three years back.' The lad stood open-mouthed in wonder. Then something seemed to occur to him, but he shook his head, as if to dismiss a doubt. Then he looked troubled again. 'Isn't it a bit early, or a bit late, for leverets?' he stammered. He wasn't as stupid as we'd all thought.

'My dear young man,' said Mick, smiling indulgently. 'The wilderness has no rules.'

'No, no, of course not,' said the lad.

As they continued up through the field, the commentary continued.

'That's where a juvenile magpie unsuccessfully chased a bank vole.' 'Look: a mistle thrush has pecked that slug. You can always tell a mistle thrush from a song thrush by the slight asymmetry of its upper and lower mandibles.' 'See where the partridges have been anting? Yes, in this weather,' he quickly added, seeing glimmerings of doubt starting to reappear. 'Even in the Antarctic winter Emperor Penguins use ants. Ants need sunlight to make Vitamin C.'

'But...', began the boy. Mick shrewdly anticipated the objection and shrugged it off.

'They're not *normal* ants, of course. They have ethylene glycol – antifreeze to you – pumping round them.'

Confident though he sounded, Mick seemed to want to change the subject.

'But here is something really interesting, at last' he said. A chain of small footprints led up beside a path and disappeared into the wood in which Mick shot at pigeons in warmer times. 'What we have here is an exotic subspecies of muntjac. Its ancestors probably came from near the border of Thailand and Burma. Let's see where he's been going.' And so they followed the prints over the fence into the wood. They paused to note where the muntjac had stopped to root for truffles. 'You get those here, do you?' asked the boy, getting bolder. Mick looked contemptuous. The question didn't need an answer. They went on, out of the field and back down towards the farm. 'An old, wandering male,' said Mick. 'In Vietnam I sometimes tracked them for hundreds of miles in the cloud forest.'

They opened the farm gate and went through. The tracks went straight across the yard to the terrier's kennel. And there they stopped. 'Interesting,' said Mick. 'This is one for a scholarly journal. Wild deer and dog co-existence: lots of mileage there.'

When the terrier bounded out, imprinting in the snow tracks identical to the ones they had followed for an hour, Mick didn't blush. There would have been no one there to embarrass him anyway. The lad, who turned out to have a zoology PhD from Cambridge, had marched off down the lane in disgust. He put his cottage near Pitney on the market that week, we heard, and went off to work for a bank near Piccadilly Circus.

36.

BADSHOT AND THE COUP DE GRÂCE

ONE DAY, Mick Badshot shot a rabbit. This was an event so unusual and improbable that it dominated the talk in the Halfway House for weeks, being displaced only by the alleged appearance in an Ilminster cafe of the ex-plumber of a Celebrity Big Brother star.

The Levels were bitterly divided about how it had happened. There was a large, loud faction that contended that the rabbit had been dead for weeks, was so badly decomposed that it had been avoided by the fastidious foxes of Isle Abbotts, and that the marks on it that Mick claimed were due to his shot were actually caused by emerging maggots. Then there were those who said that the rabbit was alive, but crippled with arthritis and heart disease, wholly unable to move, and desperate to die. And then there were those who said that there was no rabbit at all; that the whole thing was a figment of Mick's fevered imagination.

Witnesses were summoned to the bar, cross-examined, examined crossly, misrepresented and denounced. The local paper reported the dispute, putting the piece above a report of a much resented visit of the Minister of Agriculture. Blows were exchanged in a car park. A spiritualist in Taunton swore that she had been in touch with the spirit of the rabbit. It had told her, she said, that it had passed over months before, and was outraged that its skin was now being worn by Mick as a hat band. But she was found to be in the pay of the 'decomposed' faction, and after that the 'disabled' party got the upper hand.

In fact the truth was far stranger. The truth was that Mick had come into the field, seen a perfectly healthy rabbit, pointed his gun at it and pulled the trigger. The rabbit had then fallen over. Not dead, true, but dead-ish.

Mick maintained an Olympian detachment and dignity while the claims and counterclaims rolled to and fro across south Somerset. But he was well aware of what was being said, and it gave him an idea.

Shortly after the non-arrival of the ex-plumber (eventually exposed as a fairy story after some cunning detective work by one of the organisers of the 'No Tesco for Ilminster' campaign, who, having failed to keep Tesco out of the old market town, had time on his hands and zeal in his crusading heart), the good burghers of Somerset opened their morning papers to see a large advert: *'Pet Exit: Rover fetched the stick, now let him kick the bucket. Don't let your cat pine away; let it pass away. Dignified dying in a regularly disinfected van for less than the price of a black and white TV licence. Don't mess up your vehicle taking Fido for his last outing. I will "pass over" our way, usher him into eternity in a peaceful rural setting and give his mortal remains the respect they deserve.'*

What this meant was that Mick Badshot was offering a takeaway veterinary euthanasia service. He would drive round, pick up the animal, take it to the field behind his house, shoot it (or more likely shoot *at* it) and when it finally died (whether of gunshot wounds or old age), sling it in a skip.

The Levels had seen nothing like it since the Battle of Sedgemoor. The local hotel owners were deluged with enquiries from journalists and film crews. Room prices trebled. The buffet cars on First Great Western trains to Taunton sold record quantities of alcohol before breakfast as tired hacks celebrated being put onto a really interesting story for a change. And in the little lane outside Mick's house, cameramen jostled for position, elegant presenters scraped the horse dung disgustedly off their Guccis, and magpies vandalised the satellite dishes on the roofs of the broadcasting vans.

'It's an outrage' said some, including several local MPs. 'It's very enterprising,' said others, not including the local vets. 'It's very interesting,' said the solicitor who had been asked to advise whether Mick had committed an offence under the Veterinary Surgeons Act. 'We'd love to be your friend,' said almost everyone, whatever their view of the morality of the business. Because, of course, Mick was now a celebrity, and he really did exist.

For months after the media frenzy died down (which was a few weeks after it was decided that he shouldn't be prosecuted), Mick couldn't buy himself a drink. He'd stand in the midst of the adoring multitudes, sipping cider and saying sanctimoniously that he wasn't interested in the money; all he cared about was reducing the amount of suffering in the world.

The drinks lasted until Mr Gary Barlow (of 'Take That' fame) was seen buying some cheese and a newspaper in a local shop.

37.

BADSHOT
AND THE LOST YOUTH
OF ENGLAND

'WE NEED TO CATCH 'EM YOUNG,' said Mick Badshot. 'Once they get to their inner-city universities they are lost to country sports, to the countryside, and therefore to all prospects of real happiness.' He leaned on the bar, fixing with his glazed eyes the only barmaid unwise enough not to slope away at the first sign of a new lecture. 'And you, young lady,' he bellowed. 'Where would you be without the ecstasy that is the sound of a hunting horn; the thrill that is the thump of a fat wood pigeon on the grass; the deep spiritual buzz that is the whirring of a rising pheasant; the tingle that comes only from the flight of the grouse over the butts?'

'Peckham?' ventured the incautious barmaid, and ducked to avoid the pickled egg that a disgusted Mick hurled at her.

During the month that Mick was barred from the Halfway House following this incident, he pondered deeply, mostly in the shed to which Mrs Badshot had banished him for refusing to treat his athletes' foot. He would later refer to the shed as his Gulag, and to himself as the Solzhenitsyn of the field sports world. 'It was there,' he told anyone who would listen, and many people who wouldn't, 'that I had The Big Idea. It was there that The Fightback began. It was there that the hearts and minds of Young England began to turn again to the land.' And it was at this point that the hearts, minds and bodies of his audience, bemused by all the capital letters and inverted commas, generally turned away from him to the Gents, the Ladies, the car park or to any other excuse.

The Big Idea, it turned out, was to entrance infant school children with field sports by taking them out shooting, ferreting, fishing and beagling. Mick would place adverts on school notice-boards throughout South Somerset, and the children would come flocking in. They would arrive as pale, hunched, creeping, wheezing townies, clutching their Play Stations and their prejudices: they would march back, straight as Grenadiers, bold, windswept, and confident, panting only with desire to preach the gospel of the Countryside Alliance to the benighted urban heathen. Readers will remember that something like this had crossed Mick's diseased mind before, and it had all ended in tears.

But this time it seemed to work. At least for a while. Mick was right: the hunter lives in us all, and only ever dozes. He doesn't need much reawakening, even in the most inert of us, and anyone who has ever watched boys hunting as a tribe round their playground knows well that he is fully awake in young children. There was simply no competition between an offer to go shooting and the alternatives of daytime TV, the Church holiday club and kicking a ball against a piece of concrete. The kids signed up in droves in their unformed handwriting, and Mick waved the lists wildly and said 'I told you so'.

It might be said, I suppose, that Mick was a victim of his own success. To cope with the demand, Mick drew up a rota. He would take two kids out at a time for rigidly timed twenty minute sessions. These would run from eight in the morning until five in the afternoon, with an hour's break for a lunch composed of local wildlife. Since everyone in the county who held a shotgun licence had refused emphatically to have anything to do with the scheme, Mick had to do it all himself. He didn't blink. At eight on the first day he strode to the end of his drive wearing ancient tweeds and a deerstalker hat, booming to the bemused queue of denim-swathed infants and their dubious mothers: 'Come with me, numbers one and two, and I will teach you the ways of your blood-marked forefathers.' Dwight and Wayne, at the head of the queue, looked hard at each other, then at Mick, then at their mothers, and then back at Mick. 'Come, little ones, and I will turn you into killers.' That, at any rate, is what the statements of the mothers said in the investigation that followed.

The boys trotted dutifully after Mick into Mervyn's field. It was a fine day. The early spring sun of the Levels was hot on the backs of the rabbits that lay out at the edge of the wood. Rooks tumbled over the high beeches. Wood pigeons pecked away in the plough, ignoring the elaborate Croatian bird-scarer that was Mervyn's pride and joy.

Back in the queue a ripple of excitement went through the multitudes as two shots rang out. 'I hope there'll be some rabbits left for me,' said one boy. 'What a shame a gun's got only two barrels,' said another. 'They're coming back early,' said yet another.

And they were. Very fast. Dwight was screaming 'I'm deaf, I'm deaf,' and clutching his right shoulder. But he got little attention, for the star of the show was Wayne. It is amazing how fast an eight year old can run when a large ferret has his teeth sunk deep into his groin. Blood seeped out of his shell-suit trousers. The ferret swung like a huge white pendulum marking the minutes before the ambulance and the police arrived.

It didn't take long. The ambulance was mostly interested in Dwight's dislocated shoulder, for Wayne's injury turned out to be trivial. The police, on advice from their Child Protection Unit, asked some penetrating questions, in the comfort of the station, about whether it was wise to let a child start shooting with an eight bore. The queue dispersed in horror, the children and their mothers returning with renewed commitment and conviction to Sky TV and Spiderman.

38.

BADSHOT AND THE GOSHAWK

MICK BADSHOT is a man who loves kit and jargon. The jargon always comes about a fortnight before the kit, and so about a fortnight before a catastrophe. And so when we heard Mick leaning against the bar, sinking his sixth pint of matchless Somerset ale and saying dismissively of Mervyn that 'he's a man who doesn't know his bewits from his mews jesses', we all pencilled in 'Falconry Disaster' for mid-May.

'I didn't know you were a falconer,' said the Australian barmaid, bravely. Mick flushed and swelled. 'I'm not,' he said. 'I'm not and I never will be. Falconers fly falcons. I'm an austringer.' He looked round hopefully, waited to be asked what that was. There was silence. We looked into our pints. There was some embarrassed coughing and an exodus to the gents. 'An austringer,' Mick eventually declared to the remnant, 'flies hawks.'

'But you don't, do you Mick?' asked the barmaid, who was not long off the plane from Sydney, and didn't know the rules of conversation with Mick Badshot. We shot her ugly looks. She had condemned us to another red-nosed diatribe from Mick when we thought that the talk had moved happily on to the old staples: bismuth v lead: the edibility of rabbits with myxomatosis: the supremacy of the .243 for red, roe and sika: the carnage amongst local shooters associated with ham-fisted home-loading: the prospects of peace in the Middle East and, most importantly, the allegation that a Dorset ferreter had paid, with money from an illicit poteen still, for the silicone breast implants of a married bus-conductress.

'I do,' said Mick. 'I most certainly do. There is no thrill like seeing your Harris Hawk catching up with a mid-August grouse. Nothing in Mozart is as musical as the thud of your tiercel as it hits a plump wood pigeon in the back after a stoop out of the sun. But my bird is the goshawk.' He drew a deep breath and took a gulp of beer. He closed his eyes to savour it, as he'd seen on a programme about wine-tasting, and another few escapees bolted triumphantly into the car park, watched wistfully by the rest of us, who had slower reflexes.

'As you know,' he began again, 'the cornerstone of falconry and austringer literature is the *Book of St Albans*, published in 1486. And as you also know' (he looked at the gaps at the bar, more in sorrow than anger) 'that book says what hawk or falcon each rank of society should have. A Ger falcon for a king; a kestrel for a knave. But for the Yeoman' (he tapped his chest, causing a coughing fit), 'for the Yeoman, a goshawk. She arrives tomorrow

from Wolverhampton. I bought her on eBay, she is called Doris, and she is as fast as the passage of one of Mrs. Badshot's onion bhajis.' He laughed deafeningly at his own joke. He laughed alone. We were dumbstruck with boredom and horror. The horror was informed horror. Mick didn't need an airborne killing machine to wreak dreadful havoc. A tea towel was deadly in his hands.

'In Doris,' said Mick, 'ancient and modern sporting wisdom will fuse in a perfect and fecund marriage. She will be tracked with radio-telemetry, yet be schooled in the courtly French of the early Middle Ages. Her bullet jesses will be made from leather taken from the eighteenth century binding of a treatise on syphilis, but finished with ribbons made in some of Bangalore's most exploitative sweat shops.' The barmaid hastily called 'Last Orders': it was only half past nine.

Doris arrived the next day, and was duly installed in her palatial mews, fed on some dead chicks, and admired by the local youths. She performed magnificently. She looked imperiously round, kicked a chick off her perch and leapt straight onto the top of Mick's unhatted head. Mick smiled grimly as the blood ran down into his eyes. 'They often do this,' he hissed. 'It's an essential part of their bonding. She's acknowledging that we're fellow-hunters, but that I'm in charge.' Doris gripped more tightly, and the blood ran more freely. The youths looked on, open-mouthed in wonder. And then Doris did three unforgiveable things. With her beak she took hold of one of Mick's very last clumps of hair – his favourite one: the one he combs over if he's going to a Hunt Ball attended by the surgically enhanced bus-conductress – and ripped it right out. Then she covered up the newly bald patch with a neat white dollop of dung, and finally flew out over our heads. She was last seen somewhere near Bristol, flying back hard towards the land of pork scratchings.

'She's doing just fine,' said Mick, later. 'She's hacking.'

'Doesn't that mean you've let her go?' asked that curiously well-informed barmaid.

'Just for a while,' said Mick. 'It's an important part of her training.

'Oh, right,' said the barmaid, who by then had learned a bit about England.

39.

BADSHOT AND THE MORPHIC FIELD SPORTS

ROOTING THROUGH A SKIP IN CREWKERNE, Mick Badshot found a copy of one of Rupert Sheldrake's books. He dusted it off, wiped a marmalade stain from the cover ('It was first class, chunky marmalade,' said Mick. 'I'm surprised that such discriminating people should throw out a book like that') and took it home. He, the book, and a plastic jug of farm cider went into his study. He emerged the next morning, tousled and wild eyed. 'The scales have fallen from my eyes,' he declared, over the porridge. Certainly something had fallen off. 'I'll never be the same again' he assured us. Neither would any of us, as it turned out.

'It's all to do with morphic fields,' he told that long-suffering barmaid at the Halfway House. 'We are bound to everything by an invisible force. The more like us anything is, the stronger is the field that links us. We're bound to our past, and shaped by it. We tap into everything that our race has done before.'

'That's nice,' said the barmaid. 'Cheese and onion, or salt and vinegar?'

'Don't you see?' continued Mick. 'It's what Jung was saying all along. We all have access to the collective unconscious of mankind.'

'Cool,' said the barmaid. 'Pickled egg? They make me fart like a trooper, but they're worth it.'

'And not just to that of mankind,' Mick battled on, unbashed. 'To everything there is. You might have wondered why hunters are mystically linked to their prey. You might have wondered how crows know to an inch the range of a shotgun. Or how I know, without seeing, hearing or smelling, that there's a roe deer round the corner.'

'Freaky,' said the barmaid. 'That was you, wasn't it, Eric? It certainly wasn't me. Disgusting.'

From then on, morphic fields ruled our lives. Mick would try to send his beer orders by telepathy. When it didn't work, he said that the barmaid, who was from Auckland, was obviously tuned in to a different network. He knew, he said, that people were looking at the back of his head. They were, it was true, but that may have had more to do with a fascinating scar left by a visiting Australian who said he sheared sheep on his father's farm and could cut Mick's hair. He did indeed cut Mick's hair, but, since cider is stronger than Fosters, also a fair amount of Mick's skin and muscle. The haircut and the associated haemorrhage were caught on video, and for a week, until Britney knocked it off its pedestal, had the highest number of You Tube hits from the Ilminster area.

'I'm going to prove the theory once and for all,' Mick told the guests he'd invited for a barbecue and who now stood depressed in the drizzle, listening to Jimmy Osmond and looking at a charred pigeon that Mick had picked up from the A303. 'For crows, the effective range of a 12 bore is about sixty yards. With a .410 it's about forty. Now: if I change the look of the .410 so that it's identical to a 12 bore, and the crows are then happy to feed fifty yards away, we can conclude that the crows must have picked up my thoughts from the morphic field that we share.'

We were all too tired and too dispirited by the thought of that pigeon to argue. Mick went to the gun cabinet and brought out his .410. It had indeed been impressively modified. Mick had put a false barrel on over the real one, so it looked like a real 12 bore. The stock had been bulked out with plasticine, which he'd varnished.

'Good, eh?' said Mick, proudly. And it was.

'I'd like you all to witness this,' said Mick. 'This could be a turning point for science.'

In the field at the back of Mick's house there were always some crows, but Mick had never tried to shoot them before. The guests waited by the ditch at the edge of the field. Mick loaded the .410, and strode out towards a pair of feeding crows. He looked back over his shoulder to check that we were watching. We were, and an extraordinary scene unfolded.

The crows flew straight towards Mick. We heard the safety catch coming off. The crows landed, and started to walk towards Mick. Mick put the gun to his shoulder. The birds came nearer and nearer. They came within five yards of Mick, who stood, heavily armed, open-mouthed and in the epicentre of a powerful morphic field. And they looked at him. 'They're laughing,' said Mervyn. And I think he was right.

Every one of us bought Rupert Sheldrake's collected works that week.

40.

BADSHOT AND THE POWER OF SUGGESTION

IT WAS HIGH SUMMER IN THE LEVELS, and Mick Badshot was determined to make the most of it.

'It's glorious,' he boomed, mostly to himself. 'This emerald grass is what the miserably wet spring has given us to make up for its bad behaviour. Grass like that fills the heart with hope, the fields with rabbits, and the deep freeze with rabbit pie.' He was right on two out of three counts.

That night he cleaned and oiled his .22. He sat by the barbecue, cradling his .22 like a beloved child, occasionally lifting it to his shoulder and (unlike most parents cradling most beloved children), looking menacingly through the telescopic sight at the safest crows in Christendom.

'Tomorrow's going to be a good day,' he said, stroking the stock. 'No more minted chops of alleged lamb, or sausages made from noses and knackers. Tomorrow's barbecue will be a coney crematorium.'

He was up at dawn, striding martially up the lane towards Mervyn's, whistling 'Colonel Bogey', his rifle over his shoulder. He peered carefully over the gate and along the hedge. 'There they are,' he whispered. 'Their time has come.' He climbed stealthily over the gate using a technique he had learned in an SAS survival and covert surveillance manual. It was sheer bad luck that his boot got caught in the lower rung, and sheer worse luck that his outstretched hand landed on a strand of barbed wire. It was good luck, I suppose, that the barbed wire prongs were partly shielded by the cow pat that covered the wire, but by the time he hit the ground, Mick wasn't in a grateful mood. His scream and the blazing colour of his language must have shocked and woken heavily drugged rabbits with a naval background throughout the West Country. The field wobbled as feet thumped out alarms, and undulated as rabbits bolted for cover.

When the bleeding had slowed to a steady trickle, Mick picked up his blood and dung-stained gun and started to trudge back down the lane. But then he stopped. 'I wonder,' he murmured. 'I wonder. Perhaps my blood is the price I have to pay for the bag of bags.'

He peered round the hedge and turned to us with excited eyes. 'Look,' he said. 'It was meant to be.' Just fifty yards away a huge buck rabbit sat at the bottom of the hedge, its back to us, enjoying the easterly sun.

It was a textbook stalk, in the grand Highland manner. First there was the lengthy and entirely unnecessary spy with a brass telescope. Then the wind was assessed with a handful of grass. Then there was the meticulous approach, making use of all the relevant features of the landscape (a tractor tyre, a drinking trough and an abandoned Fiat Panda). And then there was the shot. Very relaxed, rifle nicely into the shoulder, resting on the game bag for maximum stability and minimum jolt. Wait for the beast to turn to you. Nothing showy; a modest but deadly heart shot. The Mohican whoop of triumph wouldn't have gone down well in some of the tweedier Highland forests, it's true, but success doesn't come often to Mick, and he can be forgiven. Nor would it be kind or relevant to point out that since the rabbit was in the last stages of myxomatosis, blind, immobile, crawling with fleas, and with testicles the size of golf balls, it wasn't the Monarch of the Glen. It duly sizzled over charcoal that night, and we generously let Mick have our portions.

The next morning Mick wandered into breakfast looking worried. 'I had an itchy night,' he told us over the porridge and prunes. We could see why. He was covered in flea bites.

'That's how myxomatosis is transmitted,' we told him. 'Watch out for those sticky eyes.'

Over the next few hours, Mick went visibly downhill. He complained of sweats, exhaustion and general malaise. He kept looking hard at himself in the top of the Aga. Five times he flicked feverishly through an entry in *Black's Veterinary Dictionary*, snapping it shut when we tried to see what he was looking at.

A moment of decision arrived. He leapt from the armchair. 'I'm just going out,' he said. 'Won't be long.'

He was wrong. He was several days. Apparently it can take that long to get things straight if you drive to a District General Hospital, go to Casualty and say that you're suffering from myxomatosis. The psychiatrists have awesome statutory powers to detain. Mick was very glad when it was sorted, even if he's known at the Canal as 'poor, sick Thumper'.

41.

BADSHOT AND THE ICELANDIC THERAPEUTIC MASSAGE

MICK BADSHOT EMERGED FROM THE GLASTONBURY FESTIVAL with a hangover, a money-making idea, and a conviction for the possession of cannabis. He was immensely proud of the conviction. He wore it like a medal. 'It's taken years off me,' he told the Halfway House, with what he thought was the knowing, salacious wink of the old dog who knows his way round the criminal underworld. 'Mick Badshot reaches parts that you lot can't even dream about.'

'But I thought you were just holding it for a stranger,' said Mervyn, unkindly. 'Someone who said that it was a pork pie.'

'Well, yes,' Mick agreed, ruefully. 'But it's the fact of the conviction that matters.'

A police officer, not from the local force, was playing darts. 'That's right,' he said, over his shoulder. 'That's right.'

The money-making idea sprang from an unhappy visit to the Healing Field. Mick, dressed in heavy flannel trousers, a baseball cap on backwards, and an Iron Maiden tee-shirt from the Taunton Oxfam shop, had strolled through in wonderment. He had sat cross-legged under pyramids, had his scalp kneaded by a fully accredited witch in a skirt made of willow-leaves, drunk water that had seeped out of one of Merlin's many tombs (this one in Utah), and, on finding that he had no money left to buy cider at Julian Temperley's famous cider bus, decided that there was a good living to be made from alternative therapies.

'There's a deep spiritual thirst,' he said. 'I will slake it. The people at the CLA Game Fair are as thirsty as anyone. I know their hearts: they are full of grief. I know their wallets: they are full of fivers. I will unburden them.'

So he hired a stall at the Game Fair. Tucked between a taxidermist and a ferret-hutch manufacturer, he was going to offer 'Icelandic Therapeutic Massage'. 'Harnessing the Healing Power of the Haddock,' his banner screamed. The idea (Mick's own) was to belabour the client around the torso with a piece of fish, while muttering some bogus Norse-ish words. There were four levels of service. Bronze, silver and gold involved respectively haddock, farmed salmon and organic salmon. A buyer of the Platinum service could take away the organic salmon used to beat him, and was presented with a certificate confirming that 'The Creature of the Salty Deep has beaten out the Creatures of the Psychic Deep.'

'Do you really think this will catch on?' said Mrs Badshot, doubtfully.

'Trust me, m'dear,' said Mick. And, bless her, despite knowing him very well, she did. She dug into her savings for the rent of the stall, bought a job lot of slightly past-its-dates haddock from Bridport, a box of sandalwood incense and a sari, and drove Mick to the Game Fair. And there, that first expectant evening, Mick and Mrs Badshot basked in the evening sun and the assurance of riches, drinking chai and doing insanely optimistic calculations of their expected profits.

Early next morning, long before the first punters arrived, they were up, sniffing the haddock, unwrapping the boxes of certificates, checking the Tibetan monastery music on the CD player, and eating bacon and eggs in the splendid catering tent.

'Morning,' said Mick to the immaculate Holland and Holland contingent, through a mouthful of Lincolnshire's finest streaky. 'Can I beat you with a fish? On the house.' They were polite young men. They looked nervously back to their kedgeree.

'Hello,' said Mick to the organiser of the Gundog Scurry. 'Such a glorious day should be greeted by a haddock around the nipples. Happy to do you after your toast and marmalade.' The organiser, who had seen a bit of life in the Gurkhas, choked and excused himself.

And then the gates were thrown open and the Great British Public came in.

The Game Fair is always wonderful, and this one was no exception. The best times are in the evenings, when the dust has settled and the crowds have abated. Then the heat and hubbub give way to cool and the chinking of glasses. Corks pop; old friends reunite; there is a happy murmuring through the site; the stories get taller as the shadows lengthen.

But this time a siren shattered the genteel calm. A blue light flashed through the avenues of the estate. In the Purdey drinks party, conversations about effortlessly enormous bags and swashbuckling transactions were adjourned. Expensively be-pearled necks strained, and elegantly be-brogued feet went up on tip-toe to see the police car screech to a halt.

'Surely they're not arresting the taxidermist?' asked a Captain of Industry.

'Perhaps an offence under the Wildlife and Countryside Act,' ventured a High Court Judge.

'No, it's not the taxidermist, or the ferret hutch woman', said a Viscount. 'It's that strange fish man.'

And it was. Mick Badshot, handcuffed and struggling, was being carried to the car. Mrs Badshot was telling an officer, through her sobs, that there was nothing sexual about the alleged assaults.

'So why get them to strip off, dear?' asked the officer, with unpleasant cynicism.

'It's the way these things are done in the Nordic world,' said Mrs Badshot, unconvincingly.

But even this unfortunate scene involved a reunion of old friends.

'You can't believe I'm guilty,' blustered Mick, from the back seat of the car.

'That'll be for the jury to decide,' said the officer, looking over his shoulder. 'It's the fact of the conviction that matters, isn't it, sir?'

42.

BADSHOT PREPARES FOR THE SEASON

IT WAS STICKY, LANGUID AND DEPRESSING IN THE LEVELS. Deep summer here was too deep. Everyone felt like an old tench. The woods felt like water weed. The pigeons were fat and tired, the rabbits couldn't be bothered to run or keep watch, but winter seemed too far off to make the foxes work hard. The keepers were on packages in Benidorm and Malaga, and the poachers arranged an informal rota system so that the lay-bys didn't get clogged and the best woods weren't dangerously crowded.

'A'al be up Highfeather tomorrow marnin'. Right by'ee, Jim?'

'That's fine, Tom. A'al not git there 'til Monday soonest. A'al be at Hassocks Copse before I take the old girl to the Clap Clinic in Taunton.'

'Bad this time, Jim?'

'Well, stops her weeding and strimming, she says.'

'That's bad. Better get her done.'

And so on.

Apart from the poachers and the discreet wing of the local hospital, there was one other hub of activity. It was the house of Mick Badshot. He was exhaustingly positive. He strode around in Empire-building khaki shorts, spouting clichés ('Time spent in reconnaissance is never wasted'; 'A stitch in time saves nine') and saying threateningly to every duck or pheasant that came over: 'Not long now: Don't get too attached to this earth, my friend.'

'August has been provided by Diana, goddess of field sports,' he said to the bemused barmaid at the Bell (he'd been barred from the Halfway House for an ugly, dangerous and indecent incident involving a chicken and mushroom pie) 'so that we can meet the autumn and her wildlife fully fit, fully armed and fully oiled.'

Mick Badshot, unfortunately, is someone who does what he says he will do. There's not a trace of saving hypocrisy in him. He waddled around the lanes near Isle Abbots in jogging pants and baseball boots; he set up his re-loading factory in the shed, until Mrs. Badshot, who has a long and scarred memory, phoned the health and safety people; he stripped down both the shotguns and then, when he couldn't put them back together again, told Mervyn that he'd devised a cunning puzzle for him; and when Mervyn had done it (two

minutes in total, with a look of contempt), oiled them both so well that big snakes of gun oil coiled out of the gun cabinet onto the shiny gun room floor.

As he walked round the house, Mick took with him an old, deactivated British Army .303 rifle which he'd point and swing at everything: flies, chickens, sheep and the postman.

'We take a dim view of that sir, to be truthful,' said the attending police officer. 'He's just got here from Manchester, and he doesn't understand our country ways.'

'Country ways?', snorted Mick, as if this would defuse the situation. 'In Manchester it must be a rare door that doesn't greet the postman with a burst from an automatic weapon.'

'I won't warn you again,' muttered the policeman, who didn't see the funny side, on the very good grounds that there wasn't one.

Mick, undeterred, crawled around hedgerows with the .22, looking through the sights at blithe, safe rabbits, and wandered to Highfeather wood, where the pigeons had learned that the thing to do, when Mick Badshot came, was to sit provocatively on the lowest branches, cooing calmly in case he didn't see them.

But on this Monday morning, the pigeons were anxious. Some had flown. The brave remnant was grumbling at the tops of the densest trees. For Jim, a man handy with a silenced rifle, was in the wood.

Mick greeted him innocently.

'Just walking, are we, Jim?' he said, for Jim had had the presence of mind to leave his rifle lying on a bed of dry sorrel when he saw Mick stumble into the wood.

'That's right, Mick,' said Jim. 'Thought I might see that old buzzard.'

'Best of luck,' said Mick, and moved on using a strange walk that he said was used by Apache stalkers, but which convinced Jim, who'd been in the St John Ambulance, that he had a scrotal hernia.

An hour later, a scream cut through the thick air and over the fields. Jim, about to squeeze the trigger, swore as the woodie rose up in panic. It sounded like a very large animal in very severe distress. And it was. Mick, putting his gun away, had slipped on the oil and gone crashing down, taking out a framed print of the Berkeley Hunt, c. 1871, a two-headed gosling in a pot of formalin, and his right wrist.

Jim stowed his pigeons and his rifle in the car, and, being a good neighbour, made his way down to Mick's to see what was up. He put his head round the door just as Mrs Badshot, shaking her head in disbelief, was bandaging the wrist.

'Best let the doctors have a look at that,' said Jim. 'I'm just taking the missus down there now. Different department, mind you. Shall I drop you?'

'You're very kind,' murmured Mick. 'Very kind.'

It wasn't the best start to the season.

43.

BADSHOT AND THE MAJESTY OF THE ENGLISH LAW

'ARE YOU MICHAEL BADSHOT?' asked the Court clerk. Mick, in his best suit, nodded solemnly.

'You are charged with an offence pursuant to section 1 of the Wildlife and Countryside Act 1981, namely that on 15 September 2009 you intentionally killed a Stock Dove, being a species protected under the said Act. Do you plead guilty or not guilty?'

Mick said nothing, but looked straight ahead, glowing with outrage.

'Do you plead guilty or not guilty?' repeated the clerk.

Mick was silent.

'Then a plea of not guilty will be entered,' said the clerk, 'and you will return here for trial.' Mick bowed to the Royal Arms above the Magistrates' bench and went home to prepare his defence.

The trouble was that there wasn't one. As soon as the corn was down, Mick had taken his decoys down to the stubble, set up a hide of astonishing sophistication and cunning, and waited. He didn't have long to wait. A little group of fat grey birds gusted in from the west, spotted the decoys, wheeled straight round and made a long, slow descent. Mick waited until they were all on the ground, pecking happily away with their backs to him, then stood up with his semi-auto at his shoulder, shouted 'Take that, you wretched Stock Doves,' and started firing manically into the birds, 'just like a Mexican bank robbery,' according to Seamus 'Shifty' Smith, plumber, poacher and principal prosecution witness, from whose statement this account is taken, and who had been crouched in a ditch across the field. At first the birds were too surprised to fly away. They floundered, flapped and blundered, and it took a while for them to take off towards Mervyn's wood. One of them never did. Confused and disoriented, it walked straight towards the hide. 'I saw Mr Badshot re-load his gun, point it at the bird, which could not have been more than five feet away, and pull the trigger,' said Shifty. 'The bird fell dead. Mr Badshot picked it up, put it in his coat pocket, dismantled the hide, and made towards his home. He appeared to be dancing and singing.'

Mervyn took off his glasses and put down Shifty's statement. 'It looks hopeless to me, Mick,' he said. 'You could tell the court about that pipe-lagging job that Shifty did for you, and about the payment dispute, but it hardly gives him a reason to hate you so much that he'd perjure himself.'

'You're right,' said Mick, mournfully. 'It looks bad. How long do you think I'll get?'

'Well,' said Mervyn, sucking his teeth, 'they take these things very seriously. I suppose if you plead guilty and throw yourself on the mercy of the court you might be out by Christmas. Not this Christmas, mind, but perhaps the one after next. It's not all bad, though. You'll learn a lot of new things about firearms, and have time to perfect your Scrabble.'

Over several pints of Otter Bright in The Canal, the defence strategy was perfected. Mick would maintain a complete and dignified silence. And so he did. He looked magnificent. His trouser creases were razor-sharp, his shoes were polished as dazzlingly as his scalp, and his bogus Royal Artillery tie lent an air of Colonial incorruptibility to the dock.

But Shifty was impressive too. He gave his evidence clearly and calmly, telling the Stipendiary Magistrate trying the case that he was an enthusiastic conservationist, that he understood perfectly that at a distance a Stock Dove might be confused with a Wood Pigeon, and, more in sorrow than anger, that he felt compelled to take the extraordinary step of reporting Mr Badshot only because it was plain that Mick knew the difference all too well.

The magistrate listened carefully and patiently to Shifty's evidence, taking copious notes. He listened carefully and respectfully to the prosecuting solicitor's submissions. He asked Mick if he wanted to say anything, and when Mick shook his head gravely, the magistrate moved straight to judgment.

He summarised the evidence neatly and accurately, and then came the verdict.

'I find Mr Smith's evidence wholly incredible. Everyone in south Somerset, if not everyone in England, knows that Mr Badshot is utterly incapable of hitting a barn door at five feet, let alone a moving target such as a' (he consulted his notes) 'Stock Dove. Not only that, it is absurd to suggest that Mr Badshot would have heard of a Stock Dove, let alone have been able to identify one. I have no hesitation in finding Mr Badshot Not Guilty. I conclude that Mr. Smith's evidence was palpably dishonest, and I shall be suggesting that he is investigated with a view to possible criminal proceedings.'

Mick was carried from the court on the shoulders of his supporters, one of whom was in lumbar traction for weeks afterwards, and another of whom had to have an operation on his knee cartilage as a result.

But Mick, strangely, did not see it as a triumph.

44.

BADSHOT AND THE HIGH BIRDS

MICK BADSHOT WAS EXCITED. A terse card had landed on the doormat, in the emphatic handwriting of the formidable Colonel Luce-Bowells, commanding Mick and his best gun to present themselves at Bowells Hall at 10 am prompt for the first pheasant drive of the season. There was no request for an RSVP: obedience was assumed. Lunch would be provided, and would be endured in stoical silence. The Bowells' lunches were known to be as grim as the shooting was wonderful. The birds were the highest in the west. So were the pork pies and the ham sandwiches. The Colonel despised modern refrigeration as he despised human weakness, the Euro, and the Channel Tunnel. 'Are you going abroad this year, Colonel?' he was asked, innocently, at a church fete. He coloured and bristled. 'Don't be ridiculous,' he thundered. 'I only ever go abroad to kill people, and for some reason that's disapproved of these days.' He turned away with parade-ground precision and stalked off to denounce the cake stall for selling fairy-cakes: 'Gives off all the wrong messages, y'know.'

Mick opened the door of his gun-cabinet, took out his beloved old AYA, stroked it tenderly, and sadly shook his head. 'It's faithful, but it won't do.' He picked up the phone to an old friend who owned a pair of Holland and Holland side-by-sides worth more than Mick's house. After a long conversation full of sycophancy and reassurance, he put the phone down with a smile of deep satisfaction.

Over the next couple of weeks tweed accessories, garters, a silver hip flask, and several pairs of cufflinks arrived in parcels with W1 postmarks. For long afternoons Mick locked himself into his bedroom, and we heard the sound of rustling, pacing and even, sometimes, mumbling: 'Yes, the old Holland and Holland does the job, Colonel', we distinctly heard him say, 'but frankly I prefer the old-fashioned methods. I've always been keen on piano-wire myself'.

At last the day dawned. Mick was up at four, polishing the borrowed gun, choosing and rejecting ties, making sure his shoes were buffed to a retina-searing guardsman's shine, and checking that the seams on his woolly socks were precisely right. Then, about three hours early, he set out in the Land Rover, waiting in a lay-by near Bowells Hall, reading about game-rearing and eating breath-freshener mints until it was time to go in.

And then the drives started. At first it all went well. Mick, confounding all the expectations of the good drinkers in The Bell, found his way to the right peg. He even went the right way when the guns circulated round the pegs. Yes, he lightly wounded a beater, but there was no absolutely conclusive evidence that it was him, and after a good deal of anxious discussion the consensus concluded, wrongly, that it was down to a visiting German in an unacceptable Loden hat. The jay's feather in the band clinched it for the Colonel, and the German (a superb, safe shot), was sent back to Heathrow in a mini-cab.

The German was fortunate. His expulsion meant that he missed lunch. But for Mick there was no escape. He shifted uneasily from one immaculate foot to the other, nervously trying his piano-wire line on the Colonel (who spluttered 'You must be a deviant, man'), and eating a grouse *vol au vent* of colossal antiquity.

That grouse, from beyond the grave, wreaked the most terrible and immediate revenge. Mick stumbled into the ancient, feudal loo, banging his head on a moose. He lay there retching, watched contemptuously by the sepia portraits of tiger-hunting colonials and their bloodthirsty memsahibs.

Amid the crashing waves of nausea there was one wave of inspiration. Whisky is anti-bacterial, isn't it?, said his memory. He reached for the brand-new, brim full hip flask. Soon the world smiled again, and so did Mick.

The whistle went for the first drive of the afternoon. Several of the guests looked pale and fragile. But Mick did not. He was red-faced and joyful. Yes, Mrs Luce-Bowells had looked icy when Mick had asked her if she had a swallow tattoo on her buttock. Yes, the local MFH had been unamused when Mick had playfully pinched his bottom. But Mick saw nothing but hilarious appreciation of his urbanity and wit.

The birds came high and fast. 'Like the Luftwaffe over Kent in the good old days', bellowed the Colonel. 'Give 'em a dose of the same medicine.' And, manfully ignoring their own gut problems, the guns blazed obediently, in the spirit of 1940. So did Mick. How happy he was. The air was thick with lead and falling birds. The gleaming Damascus barrels of the Holland and Holland were hot. The birds were safe from Mick, of course, but to himself he was a great killer.

But it all went wrong. A winged bird burst out of the wood, running fast towards Mick. Mick whooped, and fired from the hip, like Wyatt Earp. The pellets harmlessly peppered the head keeper's wax jacket. The bird came on. Mick fired again. A beater screamed and bled. The bird still came on. As if in slow motion the horrified guns on the adjacent pegs saw Mick take his Holland and Holland by the barrels, raise it above his head, and bring it smashing down just behind the vanishing tail of the pheasant. A mahogany stock makes an interesting noise when it splinters. So does a man who realises that he might have to sell his house.